ABSOLUTE BEGINNERS'

BUSINESS *Italian*

MARGARET POWELL & ROSSANA MCKEANE

D0417391

Hodder & Stoughton

A MEMBER OF THE HODDER HEADLINE GROUP

ACKNOWLEDGEMENTS

The authors and publishers would like to thank the following for permission to reproduce material in this volume:

Borghi, Trasporti Spediziona SPA p. 6; Barbarini & Foglia s.r.l. p. 6; Tre emme p. 6; Stablimento Lancio p. 10; United Airlines p. 42; Texas Instruments Italia SPA p. 43; 24 Ore SEME SPA p. 43; Gestimpresa SRL p. 43; NEC (UK) Ltd p. 43; Direzione Generale SIP pp. 43, 73, 90, 98; Valtur SPA p. 44; Ferrari UK Maranello Concessionaires Ltd p. 44; Borsa Immobiliare di Milano p. 52; CISES p. 52; Mercedes-Benz p. 56; Poltrona Frau SRL p. 57; Denivit p. 57; Parker Pen Company p. 57; Meridiana pp. 59, 67; Postal Market Catalogue Autumn–Winter 1991/92 belonging to Italian company Grande Distribuzione Avanzata SPA p. 59; BT p. 74; Italcable International Communications p. 80; Il Telefono Azzurro p. 90; Air Business Centre p. 90; Amstrad SPA p. 96; Swatch AG p. 101; Touring Giovanni p. 114; Orient Express Club p. 128; Hostarja Fuori Porta p. 128; Old West Pub p. 128; Piccolo Paradiso p. 128; Taverna Karaoke la Mamma p. 128; Rock Cafe p. 128; Galateria Gianni p. 128; Birreria p. 128; Teatro Dehon p. 128; and finally Standa SPA p. 131.

Every effort has been made to trace and acknowledge ownership of copyright. The publishers will be glad to make suitable arrangements with any copyright holders whom it has not been possible to contact.

British Library Cataloguing in Publication Data

McKeane, Rossana
  Absolute Beginners' Business Italian. –
  Coursebook. – (Absolute Beginners'
  Business Language Series)
  I. Title II. Powell, Margaret III. Series
  458.3421

ISBN 0–340–60414–X

First published 1995

Impression number	10	9	8	7	6	5	4	3
Year			2003	2002	2001	2000		

Typeset by Wearset, Boldon, Tyne and Wear.
Printed in Great Britain for Hodder & Stoughton Educational, a division of Hodder Headline Plc, 338 Euston Road, London NW1 3BH by J. W. Arrowsmith Ltd., Bristol.

CONTENTS

Introduction   **page v**

CAPITOLO UNO   **In arrivo**   **page 1**

Formal greetings; checking into a hotel;
enquiring about public transport; giving
simple information about yourself.

Pronunciation; asking questions; *sono, è,
ho, ha*; masculine and feminine noun
endings; some definite articles; indefinite
articles; *–are* verbs, two forms only;
numbers 1–20; adding hundreds and
thousands.

CAPITOLO DUE   **In ufficio**   **page 23**

Meeting new colleagues; finding your
way around; getting to know who does
what; taking a break; talking informally.

Making introductions; the definite article
continued; asking questions with *dove?
chi? che cosa?*; numbers 20–40; some
prepositions; some adjectives; *–ire* verbs,
three forms only; using the informal form
of the verb; more forms of *essere* and *avere*;
fare and *venire*.

CAPITOLO TRE   **La giornata lavorativa**   **page 47**

Finding out about office routine and
exactly what people do; using the 24-hour
clock; saying what you are interested in.

–are, –ere, and *–ire* verbs, more forms;
conoscere, potere and *volere*; negatives;
asking questions with *quanto?*; days of the
week; morning, afternoon and evening;
saying 'it', 'him' and 'her'.

CAPITOLO QUATTRO   **Al lavoro**   **page 71**

Using office equipment; saying that things
are not working; saying that you do not
know how to do something; asking for
help when things go wrong; finding out
how people are.

Instructions; *basta* and *bisogna*; *dovere*;
sapere; more prepositions; the alphabet;
questions with *come? perché?*; *mi dispiace
ma*; *mi interessa*.

CAPITOLO CINQUE   **Lavorare da solo**   **page 93**

Using the company's database; phoning
for assistance; sorting out a problem;
helping a visitor.

mi può, mi puoi?; imperative negative; *più
di, meno di, come*; countries in the EU; *che
bello!*

CAPITOLO SEI   **Fuori ufficio**   **page 111**

Talking about yourself; enquiring about
people's background; getting information
about services and accommodation;
ordering a meal; expressing your thanks.

da quanto tempo?; *mi piacerebbe . . .* ;
vorrei . . . ; more verb forms; money; letter
writing conventions.

Note
When a verb is used, it is marked with an asterisk and the infinitive form, the
form of the verb you would find in a dictionary, is supplied in brackets. This is
done so that the student can look up the verb easily in the Glossary and, if
necessary, be referred to the appropriate section of the book for further
information.

Series Editor's Introduction

WHO IS THE *ABSOLUTE BEGINNERS'* SERIES FOR?

The *Absolute Beginners'* series of business language courses has been designed to meet two major, but related, requirements. One is the need many adult learners now have for competence in a foreign language in an occupational setting. The other is the need teachers have for introductory language courses aimed at the true beginner.

The objectives of the series are, therefore, to provide a thorough grounding in the basics of the language, while concentrating on the situations and vocabulary needs of someone working in a foreign business environment. As such, the *Absolute Beginners' Business Language* series will be of value in higher education, particularly in institution-wide language programmes, as well as in further and adult education. Members of the business community will find the series a useful introduction to other courses with a more pronounced business focus; teachers in secondary education may also wish to consider the series as an alternative to general language courses at post-16 level.

WHAT DOES THE SERIES COVER?

Each book in the *Absolute Beginners'* series follows the experiences of a student from the UK taking up a work placement in a foreign company. In the course of the first working day, the student is introduced to new colleagues, and gradually gets to know the office, the department and the working routine of the company. Other situations covered include such things as making appointments, escorting visitors, showing someone round the company, telephoning and sending a fax, taking messages, coping when things go wrong, visiting the canteen and socialising with colleagues. By the end of the course, students will have a thorough grounding in the basics of the language, in terms of grammar and a range of standard work vocabulary, as well as active practice in using the language in context via exercises designed particularly to develop listening comprehension and speaking skills.

HOW IS THE COURSE STRUCTURED?

Each book in the series consists of six chapters, each based on four short dialogues illustrating a typical working situation and introducing and/or reinforcing a key language point. The exercises following the dialogues provide a range of varied activities which develop receptive skills, including listening comprehension, and establish the basis for active speaking practice in the form of pairwork, role-plays and dialogue chains. Grammar points have been fully integrated into the text; as new grammar is introduced in the dialogues, brief explanations are given, followed by exercises offering further practice of the point concerned. Each chapter finishes with a detailed checklist of the language and communication skills covered. At the back of the book there is a comprehensive glossary with English equivalents.

The *Absolute Beginners'* series provides extensive opportunities for listening to and using the spoken language. All the dialogues and many of the exercises have been recorded on two C60 cassettes, available together with a Support Book containing the cassette transcripts and key to exercises.

RECOMMENDED COURSE LENGTH, ENTRY AND EXIT LEVELS

It is obviously difficult to specify precisely how much time it would take to complete a course in the *Absolute Beginners'* series, as individual classroom circumstances can vary so widely. Taken at a steady pace, the course can be completed in one 15-week semester, assuming a minimum of two hours' class contact per week and regular directed study. For many teaching colleagues, this could be an attractive option, but there would be very little time to incorporate other materials or activities. More conventionally, the course can be completed comfortably within an academic year, again assuming a minimum of two hours' class contact per week and regular directed study. On this basis, teachers would find that they had some time to devote to extending the range of language and situations covered and thus give the course an additional business or general focus.

As the series title indicates, the course is designed for learners with no prior knowledge of the language and it proceeds at their pace. The range of language, situations and grammar is deliberately modest, but this range is covered very thoroughly in order to lay sound foundations for subsequent language learning. The course has not been designed with the needs of any particular examinations syllabus in mind; rather, in writing the coursebooks in the series, authors have been guided by NVQ Level 1 standards for language competence at work, as defined by the Languages Lead Body.

THE *ABSOLUTE BEGINNERS'* SERIES AND THE *HOTEL EUROPA* SERIES

The *Absolute Beginners'* series acknowledges the debt it owes to the *Hotel Europa* series. Though a free-standing course in its own right, *Absolute Beginners'* utilises some of the same characters and settings from *Hotel Europa*; for example, the student is placed in the company which is the customer for the hotel's conference and accommodation facilities in *Hotel Europa*. Similarly, the approach in *Absolute Beginners'* mirrors that in *Hotel Europa* by basing the series on realistic working situations, accessible to teacher and learner alike, whatever their business background. Teachers using *Absolute Beginners'* and looking for a course to help their students to progress will find that *Absolute Beginners'* provides an excellent introduction to *Hotel Europa* and that the transition will be smooth.

ACKNOWLEDGEMENTS

On behalf of all the authors involved with the *Absolute Beginners'* series I should like to acknowledge the invaluable contribution of Tim Gregson-Williams and his team at Hodder & Stoughton to realising the concept for this series, and to thank the many colleagues and course participants – sadly too numerous to mention here – who have provided us with feedback and suggestions. We have very much appreciated their views and thank them all for their assistance.

Marianne Howarth
Department of Modern Languages
The Nottingham Trent University

In arrivo
ARRIVING

In this chapter you will learn how to:
- meet somebody for the first time
- check into a hotel
- enquire about public transport
- give simple information about yourself

PRESENTAZIONI

Nome: Michael
Cognome: Moor
Nazionalità: inglese
Età: 20 anni

Nome: Simonetta
Cognome: Giorgi
Nazionalità: italiana
Età: 26 anni

DIALOGO 1 *All'aeroporto*

Michael Moor arriva* all'aeroporto di Bologna. (*arrivare)

Michael Moor arrives at Bologna Airport, and is met by Simonetta Giorgi, personal assistant to the sales director at Italsistemi.

 Studiate queste espressioni, ascoltatele e ripetetele nelle pause previste. *Study these expressions, listen and repeat them in the pause provided.*

scusi	*excuse me (polite form)*
piacere	*pleased (to meet you)*
com'è andato il viaggio?	*how did the journey go?*
bene, grazie	*fine, thanks*
allora	*well then*
andiamo?* (andare)	*shall we go?*
d'accordo	*OK*

 Adesso chiudete il libro e ascoltate il dialogo. *Now close your book and listen to the dialogue.*

SIMONETTA GIORGI: Scusi, Lei è il signor Moor?
MICHAEL MOOR: Sì, Mike Moor.
SIMONETTA GIORGI: Sono Simonetta Giorgi . . . Piacere.
MICHAEL MOOR: Piacere.
SIMONETTA GIORGI: Com'è andato il viaggio?
MICHAEL MOOR: Bene, grazie.
SIMONETTA GIORGI: Allora, andiamo?
MICHAEL MOOR: D'accordo.

Ascoltate il dialogo di nuovo, questa volta con il libro aperto. Usate il tasto pausa e ripetete ogni frase. *Listen to the dialogue again, this time with your book open. Pause the cassette and repeat each phrase.*

GRAMMATICA

sono   *I am*
è   *you are*

In Italian, you do not usually use the words for 'I' and 'you' etc. unless you need them for emphasis. Simonetta checks that she has the right person by saying: *Lei è il Signor Moor?* 'Are **you** Mr Moor?'

Lei   *you (polite or formal)*

ESERCIZIO 1.1

Practise the dialogue with a partner making sure your pronunciation is correct. Retaining the same role, move to another partner and practise again. When you are sure you can do this without the book, change roles and repeat the process.

DA NOTARE   *Asking questions*

The simplest way of asking a question in Italian is to change your intonation by raising your voice at the end of a sentence.

 ### ESERCIZIO 1.2

Listen to the cassette and see if you can decide whether the following are questions or statements:

	1	2	3	4	5	6
Question						
Statement						

 ### ESERCIZIO 1.3

Look at the following words. You have probably heard or seen them all before. But could you pronounce them as an Italian would? Listen to them on cassette and repeat them in the spaces provided.

Ferrari   orchestra   spaghetti   cinema   Giorgio Armani
Pavarotti   Roma   scenario   scientifico catalogo   centro

DA NOTARE *Pronunciation*

'c' is normally pronounced 'k' but when followed by 'i' or 'e' is pronounced 'ch' e.g. *cinema, centro*.

But remember that 'ch' in Italian is always pronounced 'k' and **never** 'ch' as in English!

Similarly, 'sc' is normally pronounced 'sk' but when followed by 'i' or 'e' is pronounced 'sh' e.g. *scientifico, scenario*.

And 'g' is normally pronounced 'g' as in 'got' but when followed by 'i' or 'e' is pronounced 'j' e.g. *Giorgio, genetico*.

Now look at *Esercizio 1.3* once again.

ESERCIZIO 1.4

Study the list of questions and expressions on the left and join them to the correct response from the list on the right.

1 Com'è andato il viaggio?	a No, sono Bob Williams
2 Andiamo?	b Piacere
3 Piacere	c Bene, grazie
4 Lei è il signor Moor?	d D'accordo

DA NOTARE *Forms of address*

Mr signor(e)   *Mrs* signora   *Miss* signorina

When you address someone directly, you will say: *Buongiorno, signor Verdi*, but if you are talking about someone or checking if the person you are talking to is the person you want, you have to say:

il signor Verdi   la signora Denti   la signorina Giorgi

ESERCIZIO 1.5

Work with a partner. On different occasions you are asked to go to the airport to meet the following people. Each time you will have to check that you have got the right person. Your partner will take the part of the person arriving. Swop roles and try the exercise again.

Modello

LEI: Scusi, Lei è il signor Giorgi?
SERGIO: Sì, Sergio Giorgi.
LEI: Sono .... (*supply your name*). Piacere . . .
SERGIO: Piacere.

Signor Mario Denti

Signora Carla Bini

Signorina Marta Rossi

Signor Paolo Verdi

ESERCIZIO 1.6

For further practice, mingle with other members of your class and check who they are or that you have remembered their names correctly.

ESERCIZIO 1.7

PROTEGGI  ASSICURA

a
Manomissioni, introduzioni, sottrazioni illegali

b
Aperture accidentali e perdite di oggetti

c
Danneggiamenti, abrasioni e lacerazioni

d
Linea telefonica per informazioni viaggio e assistenza polizza

e
Recapito ovunque di una propria valigia sostitutiva

f
Massimale di 500 $ per danneggiamento o furto parziale

Sometimes it is necessary to make educated guesses when trying to understand a foreign language. Look carefully at the pictures on p. 5 and their Italian captions. Match the English captions below to their Italian counterparts.

1 Accidental opening and loss of contents.
2 Forwarding of replacement case to any destination.
3 Travel information and policy help line.
4 Reimbursement of up to $500 for damage or partial theft.
5 Illegal interference, addition or removal of items.
6 Damage, scratching and tearing.

ESERCIZIO 1.8

From the above Italian captions, choose the ones that look like English words and write down their English equivalents. Check your answers in the glossary at the back of the book.

ESERCIZIO 1.9

Study the three advertisements below and write down the things that the companies have in common.

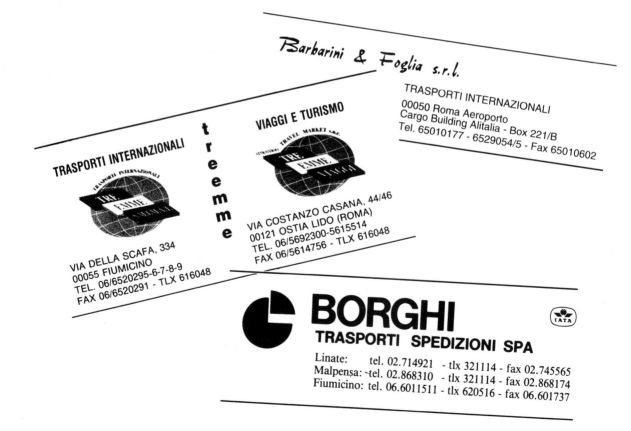

DIALOGO 2   *In albergo*

Simonetta Giorgi accompagna* Michael Moor all'albergo.
(*accompagnare)

ALBERGO

Simonetta Giorgi takes Michael Moor to the hotel.

PRESENTAZIONE

Sono Gianfranco Gentile. Sono portiere all'Hotel Europa. Ho vent' anni.

 Studiate queste espressioni, ascoltatele e ripetetele nelle pause previste.

buongiorno	*good morning/good day*
questo è* (essere)	*this is*
per la Italsistemi?	*for the Italsistemi company?*
vero?	*isn't it? (literally: true?)*
una singola	*a single room*
con bagno	*with bath*
ecco	*here is*
la chiave	*the key*
la camera	*the room*
ha?* (avere)	*have you got?*
un documento	*a means of identification*
per favore	*please*

Adesso chiudete il libro e ascoltate il dialogo.

PORTIERE:	Buongiorno, signorina, signore.
SIMONETTA GIORGI:	Buongiorno. Questo è il signor Michael Moor.
PORTIERE:	Ah, sì. Per la Italsistemi, vero?
SIMONETTA GIORGI:	Sì. Una singola con bagno.
PORTIERE:	Ecco la chiave. È la camera numero tre.
MICHAEL MOOR:	Grazie.
PORTIERE:	Ha un documento, per favore?
MICHAEL MOOR:	Sì, ho il passaporto.

Ascoltate il dialogo di nuovo, questa volta con il libro aperto. Usate il tasto pausa e ripetete ogni frase.

GRAMMATICA

Essere and *avere*

essere   *to be*

È, è   means 'is', 'it is', 'he is', 'she is' or as we have already seen 'you are' whereas *E, e* (no accent) means 'and'

avere   *to have*

ho   *I have*
ha?   *have you got?* or *has she/he got?*
ha   *you have, she/he/it has,* or just *has*

NB You say *Ho vent'anni* 'I have twenty years' and not 'I am twenty'.

ESERCIZIO 2.1

Practise the dialogue with two partners making sure your pronunciation is correct. Retaining the same role, move to another set of partners and practise again. When you are sure you can do this without the book, change roles and repeat the process. Do this as many times as you need.

ESERCIZIO 2.2

This is the form the hotel receptionist will have to fill in for you. Try filling it in yourself.

Scheda di notificazione

Nome: _____

Cognome: _____

Nazionalità: _____

Indirizzo: _____

Numero del passaporto: _____

Data di scadenza: _____

ESERCIZIO 2.3

Listen to the cassette and repeat the numbers zero to 10 in the gaps provided.
Do this several times.

ESERCIZIO 2.4

What are the following numbers in English? Rewrite them in the correct order
in Italian.

tre   uno   sette   otto   due   cinque   dieci   sei   nove   quattro   zero

ESERCIZIO 2.5

Now, listen to the cassette and repeat the numbers 11 to 20 in the gaps
provided. Do this until you feel sure of them.

DA NOTARE

Venti is 20, but when it is followed by a vowel, the final 'i' is replaced by an
apostrophe e.g. *ho vent'anni*.

ESERCIZIO 2.6

What are the following numbers in English? Rewrite them in the correct order
in Italian.

diciassette   quindici   sedici   diciannove   diciotto   venti   tredici
dodici   undici   quattordici

DA NOTARE

It will be essential to be able to talk in hundreds and thousands when dealing
with Italian currency. You simply add the word *cento* for a hundred or
hundreds, *mille* for a thousand and *mila* for thousands, as below:

mille	1000	cento	100	millecento	1100
duemila	2000	duecento	200	duemiladuecento	2200
tremila	3000	trecento	300	tremilatrecento	3300
quattromila	4000	quattrocento	400	quattromilaquattrocento	4400

li 15/10 1995   lit. 1000.000

NGB 3476-9   02 MILANO
C.A.B. 18721-19
06- 77.192.0246-09

a vista pagate per questo
(Assegno Bancario)

lire   *1 milione*

all'ordine   *Rossi Giovani*

Carlo Bianchi

182435/6/95

-0146057485= 5633010>

Officina carte valori Milano
imp. bollo virtuale Autorizz.
int. Fin. Milano n 18 del 1970

How much is this cheque for?

ESERCIZIO 2.7

Use the cassette for further pronunciation practice.

ESERCIZIO 2.8

Quanto costa? How much does it cost? Look at the price list below and answer the questions.

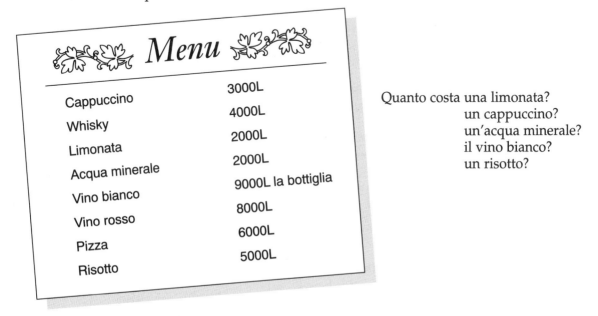

Menu

Cappuccino	3000L
Whisky	4000L
Limonata	2000L
Acqua minerale	2000L
Vino bianco	9000L la bottiglia
Vino rosso	8000L
Pizza	6000L
Risotto	5000L

Quanto costa una limonata?
  un cappuccino?
  un'acqua minerale?
  il vino bianco?
  un risotto?

ESERCIZIO 2.9

Below you will find the names, addresses and telephone numbers of 10 airline companies.

BALKAN AIRLINES (LZ) *Viale Gorizia, 14* *00198 Roma -* ☎ **8417371**	GARUDA (GA) *Via Barberini, 97* *00187 Roma -* ☎ **4821693**
BIMAN BANGLADESH AIRLINES (BG) *Via Lucullo, 3* *00187 Roma -* ☎ **4819041**	GHANA AIRWAYS (GH) *Via Sicilia, 50* *00187 Roma -* ☎ **4885140**
BRITISH AIRWAYS (BA) *Via Bissolati, 76* *00187 Roma -* ☎ **47171**	GULF AIR (GF) *Via Barberini, 11* *00187 Roma -* ☎ **4881416**
CAMEROON AIRLINES (UY) *Via Bissolati, 20* *00187 Roma -* ☎ **4872207**	IBERIA (IB) *Via Bertoloni, 3/D* *00197 Roma -* ☎ **1678-25114 / 1678-31055**
CANADIAN AIRLINES INTERNATIONAL (CP) *Via Barberini, 3* *00187 Roma -* ☎ **4883514**	IRAN AIR (IR) *Via Bissolati, 55* *00187 Roma -* ☎ **4741141/2/3/4**

Listen to the cassette and decide which airline companies are being called.

In real life, you can always ask someone to repeat: *Ripeta, per favore* or make them slow down by repeating the numbers after them.

ESERCIZIO 2.10

Look at the above list of airlines. The person on the cassette will ask you what the number is for five of them and you must reply.

Modello   Domanda: Qual'è il numero di telefono della Gulf Air?
            Risposta: Quattro otto otto quattro uno sei.

DA NOTARE   *Nouns*

Nouns are the names we give people, things or concepts e.g. 'secretary', 'company', 'reliability' and they can be either masculine or feminine in Italian.

Nouns ending in 'o' are usually masculine.
Nouns ending in 'a' are usually feminine.
Nouns ending in 'e', some are masculine, some are feminine and this has to be learnt, e.g. *nome* is masculine but *chiave* is feminine.

GRAMMATICA   *How to say 'the'*

The word for 'the' changes according to whether a noun is masculine or feminine:

masculine singular	**feminine singular**
il e.g. il passaporto	la e.g. la camera
Nouns beginning with a vowel or 'h'	
l' e.g. l'hotel	l' e.g. l'acqua *(water)*

NB *La Italsistemi* is an exception because in fact it is short for *la (società) Italsistemi*. You will see other examples of company names beginning with a vowel.

ESERCIZIO 2.11

What would you put in front of the following nouns: *il, l'* or *la*?

passaporto	camera	documento
signora	singola	nome
signore	numero	signorina
aeroporto	chiave	albergo
uscita	viaggio	indirizzo
orchestra	acqua minerale	

GRAMMATICA   *How to say 'a', 'an'*

With masculine nouns: *un*.
With feminine nouns: *una*, but *un'* followed by a vowel or 'h' e.g. *un'agenzia*.

ESERCIZIO 2.12

Look at *Esercizio 2.11* and decide whether you would use *un, un'* or *una* with each of the nouns listed.

DA NOTARE   *Hotel words*

una singola
una doppia
con bagno
con doccia
con due letti

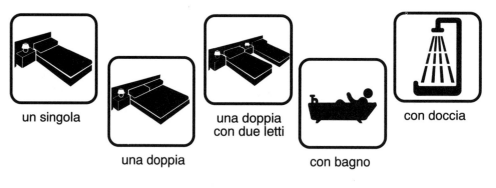

un singola   una doppia   una doppia con due letti   con bagno   con doccia

---

ESERCIZIO 2.13

Work with a partner. One of you will take the part of a hotel receptionist and the other will book the rooms as indicated below.

Modello

PORTIERE: Buongiorno.
LEI: Buongiorno, ha una doppia con bagno, per favore?
PORTIERE: Sì, la camera numero tre. Ha un documento?
LEI: Sì, ho il passaporto.

DIALOGO 3 *In autobus*

Michael cerca* un autobus. (*cercare)

Michael looks for a bus.

🔲 Studiate queste espressioni, ascoltatele e ripetetele nelle pause previste.

c'è,	*there is*
c'è?	*is there?*
dov'è?	*where is?*
la fermata	*the bus stop*
per piacere	*please*
qui	*here*
a destra	*on the right*
il biglietto	*the ticket*
un'edicola	*a news-stand (where you can buy bus tickets)*
a sinistra	*on the left*
prego	*don't mention it*

🔲 Adesso chiudete il libro e ascoltate il dialogo.

MICHAEL MOOR: Scusi, c'è un autobus per via Mazzini?
PORTIERE: Sì, il numero 9.
MICHAEL MOOR: Dov'è la fermata, per piacere?
PORTIERE: È qui a destra.
MICHAEL MOOR: E per il biglietto?
PORTIERE: C'è un'edicola qui a sinistra.
MICHAEL MOOR: Grazie.
PORTIERE: Prego.

Ascoltate il dialogo di nuovo, questa volta con il libro aperto. Usate il tasto pausa e ripetete ogni frase.

GRAMMATICA   *dov'è?* – where is?

dov' is shortened from *dove* meaning 'where' because it is followed by the vowel '*è*'.

ESERCIZIO 3.1

Practise the dialogue with a partner making sure your pronunciation is correct. Retaining the same role, move to another partner and practise again. When you are sure you can do this without the book, change roles and repeat the process.

ESERCIZIO 3.2

Which would you use in the following sentences: *c'è* or *è*?

1 .... un autobus per via Mazzini?
2 Questo .... il signor Michael Moor.
3 Lei .... la signorina Giorgi?
4 .... un'edicola qui a sinistra.
5 La fermata .... qui a destra.

Do you know what each sentence means?

ESERCIZIO 3.3

Look at these other means of transport.

TRASPORTI
AEREI
Un volo

TRASPORTI
FERROVIARI
Un treno

TRASPORTI
AUTOSTRADALI
Un pullman

TRASPORTI
URBANI
Un tram

Un autobus

Modello   Stimolo: Ask if there is a train to Parma.
Risposta: C'è un treno per Parma?

Ask if there is a . . .
1 Train to Rome
2 Flight to Palermo
3 Coach to Pisa
4 Tram to Piazza della Repubblica
5 Bus to Via Mazzini

When you need to ask questions of this kind it is useful to have a notebook ready for difficult replies and ask people to write down times: *Me lo scriva, per favore.*

DA NOTARE   *Directions*

a sinistra   dritto   a destra

ESERCIZIO 3.4

Can you work out what the following signs mean? Match the words in the left-hand column with the meanings on the right.

1 Uscita	a Way-in
2 Informazioni	b Bus stop
3 Entrata	c News-stand
4 Fermata – bus	d Car-hire
5 Edicola	e Taxi service airport – town
6 Servizio taxi aeroporto – città	f Exit
7 Noleggio auto	g Information
8 Prenotazioni	h Bookings

ESERCIZIO 3.5

Listen to the directions on the cassette and answer the questions below.

Which way would you go:
1 If you wished to leave the building?
2 To find something out?
3 If you needed to collect the key to your room?
4 If you needed to wash your hands?
5 If you wanted to make a phone call?

ESERCIZIO 3.6

You have to find your way to the *Olivetti* office in *Via Verdi.* Is there a bus? Listen to the whispered prompts and ask the appropriate questions.

ESERCIZIO 3.7

During your stay in Italy you hope to visit the following people. As soon as you get to the town you check whether or not there is a bus to the address indicated. Listen to the replies on cassette and jot down the information you receive in the grid below.

Modello

PORTIERE: Buongiorno. Desidera?
LEI: C'è un autobus per Via di Porta Pinciana, per favore?
PORTIERE: No, ma c'è il tram, il numero diciassette.

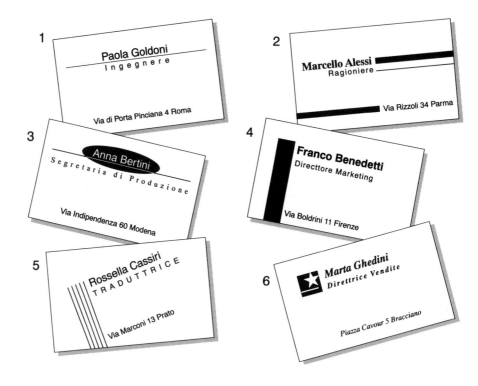

1 Paola Goldoni
  Ingegnere
  Via di Porta Pinciana 4 Roma

2 Marcello Alessi
  Ragioniere
  Via Rizzoli 34 Parma

3 Anna Bertini
  Segretaria di Produzione
  Via Indipendenza 60 Modena

4 Franco Benedetti
  Direttore Marketing
  Via Boldrini 11 Firenze

5 Rossella Cassiri
  TRADUTTRICE
  Via Marconi 13 Prato

6 Marta Ghedini
  Direttrice Vendite
  Piazza Cavour 5 Bracciano

Means of transport	Number	Extra information
1 Via di Porta Pinciana		
2 Via Rizzoli		
3 Via Indipendenza		
4 Via Boldrini		
5 Via Marconi		
6 Piazza Cavour		

DA NOTARE Remember that you have to buy your bus/tram/metro ticket before you get on and that it only becomes valid when you punch it in the machine on the vehicle. Tickets are available from newsagents and tobacconists and it is advisable to buy a block: *un blocchetto.*

ESERCIZIO 3.8

Look carefully at the tickets and answer the questions below.

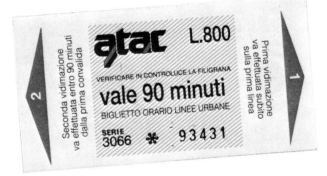

1 For how long is this ticket valid?
2 How much does it cost?
3 How many times can you use it?
4 Can it only be used on town services?

5 When is this ticket valid?

6 Where would you use this ticket?

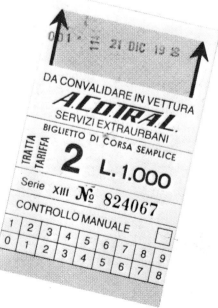

DIALOGO 4   *In ufficio*

Michael Moor arriva in ufficio.

Michael Moor arrives at the office.

PRESENTAZIONE

Sono Aldo Ruffini. Sono italiano e lavoro per la Italsistemi. Sono portiere.

 Studiate queste espressioni, ascoltatele e ripetetele nelle pause previste.

buonasera	*good afternoon, evening (the greeting you use from about 4.30 onwards)*
desidera?* (desiderare)	*how may I help? (lit: you desire?)*
da Londra	*from London*
per fare tirocinio	*to do work experience*
un attimo	*one moment*
pronto	*hello (but only when answering the phone)*
va* bene (andare)	*OK*
arrivo* subito (arrivare)	*I am coming immediately.*
tutto bene?	*everything OK?*
molto bene	*very well*

Adesso chiudete il libro e ascoltate il dialogo.

PORTIERE:	Buonasera. Desidera?
MICHAEL MOOR:	Buonasera. Sono Michael Moor. Arrivo da Londra.
	Sono qui per fare tirocinio.
PORTIERE:	Ah sì, con la signorina Giorgi. Un attimo, telefono . . .
SIMONETTA GIORGI:	Pronto?
PORTIERE:	Signorina Giorgi, qui c'è un signore per Lei da Londra.
SIMONETTA GIORGI:	Va bene. Arrivo subito.
SIMONETTA GIORGI:	Buonasera, Michael. Tutto bene?
MICHAEL MOOR:	Sì, grazie, molto bene.

ASCENSORE

Ascoltate il dialogo di nuovo, questa volta con il libro aperto. Usate il tasto pausa e ripetete ogni frase.

ESERCIZIO 4.1

Practise the dialogue with two partners making sure your pronunciation is correct. Retaining the same role, move to another set of partners and practise again. When you are sure you can do this without the book, change roles and repeat the process. Do this as many times as you need.

GRAMMATICA

arrivare – to arrive

A verb is an action or state of being. It tells you what people are doing, thinking or feeling. Being able to distinguish a verb from a noun in Italian is very important because, in the case of the verb, the last letter or letters tell you who or what is doing the action. This is because Italians do not need to use 'I', 'you', 'he', 'she', 'it', 'we', 'they'; whereas in the case of a noun (see definition on p. 11), the final letter tells you whether it is masculine or feminine, singular or plural.

arrivare is a verb meaning 'to arrive' and when it changes to *arrivo* the 'o' on the end indicates who is arriving – in this case – 'I am arriving' or 'I arrive'. An 'a' on the end can mean several things depending on the context: 'you are arriving' or 'you arrive' or 'he is arriving' or 'he arrives' or 'she is arriving' or 'she arrives' or 'it is arriving' or 'it arrives'.

L'arrivo is a noun meaning 'the arrival'. Nouns can only be masculine or feminine, singular or plural. The final 'o' in this case indicates that *l'arrivo* is a masculine singular noun. Most often nouns are preceded by *il, la l'*, *un, una* etc. You will see that in the vocabulary at the end of the book, a noun is indicated by (n) and a verb by an asterisk.

NB If you look in a dictionary, you will find 'arrive' listed as *arrivare*. Most verbs which end in *are* will follow the above pattern.

ESERCIZIO 4.2

Which would you use in the following sentences *arrivo* or *arriva*?

Modello   You have just arrived from Rome.
        Arrivo da Roma.

1 You have just arrived at Bologna from London.
    ……… da Londra.
2 You know that Simonetta Giorgi is arriving at London airport.
    Simonetta Giorgi ……… all'aeroporto di Londra.
3 You wish to tell someone you will be there straight away.
    ……… subito.
4 You know that Michael is arriving with Paolo.
    Michael ……… con Paolo.

ESERCIZIO 4.3

Up to now we have seen that:

per   means 'for' or 'in order to'
da   means 'from'
con   means 'with'

Which would you use in the following sentences *per, da* or *con*?

1 Sono qui ……… fare tirocinio.
2 Michael Moor arriva ……… Londra.
3 Ha il documento ……… Matteo?
4 Michael arriva ……… Simonetta.
5 C'è un autobus ……… via Mazzini?

ESERCIZIO 4.4

Read the following passage and see if you can understand what it means.

Michael Moor arriva a Bologna da Londra. È inglese. Ha vent'anni. È qui per fare tirocinio alla Italsistemi, in Via Mazzini. Simonetta Giorgi accompagna Michael all'Hotel Europa, dove ha una camera singola con bagno. Per andare alla Italsistemi, cerca un autobus. È il numero nove. La fermata è a destra, davanti all'albergo e per fortuna, c'è un'edicola a sinistra per il biglietto. Michael compra un blocchetto. Arriva in ufficio. È molto contento. Tutto va bene.

ESERCIZIO 4.5

You arrive at the airport and you know that Simonetta Giorgi will be meeting you at the exit. What do you say in reply to her questions?

Listen to the cassette and answer the questions in the pauses provided. The prompts will help you decide what to say. Listen to the correct answer and repeat it.

SIMONETTA GIORGI: Scusi, Lei è qui per fare tirocinio alla Italsistemi?
LEI: *Yes, my name is. . . . (What will you say as you shake hands?)*
SIMONETTA GIORGI: Ah piacere. Simonetta Giorgi. Com'è andato il viaggio?
LEI: *Very well, thank you.*
SIMONETTA GIORGI: Allora, andiamo.
LEI: *OK, let's go.*

ESERCIZIO 4.6

You arrive at the hotel and ask for a room.

SIMONETTA GIORGI: Ecco l'Hotel Europa.
PORTIERE: Buongiorno, signori.
LEI: *Good day.*
PORTIERE: Desidera?
LEI: *Do you have a single room with bath?*
PORTIERE: Vediamo. Sì, la camera numero dodici. Ha un documento, per favore?
LEI: *Give the appropriate answer.*
PORTIERE: Grazie. Ecco la chiave.

ESERCIZIO 4.7

You need to find out if there is a bus to the Italsistemi offices.

ITALSISTEMI ★

Italsistemi S.p.A.
40122 Bologna
Via Mazzini 153
Telefono: 051/399844
Telefax: 051/39835276

PORTIERE: Buongiorno, signore.
LEI: *Hello, is there a bus for via Mazzini?*
PORTIERE: No, ma c'è il tram, il numero sei.
LEI: *Where is the stop?*
PORTIERE: È subito qui a destra.
LEI: *Where can I buy a ticket?*
PORTIERE: C'è un'edicola qui a sinistra.
LEI: *Thank you.*

ESERCIZIO 4.8

Listen to the prompts on cassette and see if you can give the information required about yourself.

Prima di continuare

Before going on to the next chapter, make sure that you know how to:

• exchange greetings with somebody	*buongiorno, signore* *piacere*
• check that you are speaking to the right person	*Lei è la signorina Giorgi?*
• introduce yourself	*sono Michael Moor da Londra*
• check into a hotel	*una singola con bagno*
• find out if there is public transport to your destination	*c'è un autobus per Via Mazzini?*
• give simple information about yourself	*sono inglese* *ho vent'anni* *sono qui per fare tirocinio*
• ask essential questions	*com'è? dov'è? quanto costa? qual'è?*
• express agreement	*d'accordo/va bene*
• understand simple directions	*a destra/a sinistra/dritto*

In ufficio
IN THE OFFICE

In this chapter you will:
- meet new colleagues
- find your way around the building
- get to know who does what
- take a well-earned break

Che lavoro fa*? (fare)

SEZIONE COMMERCIALE

Direzione commerciale
Matteo Cerulli
è il direttore commerciale

Segretaria di direzione
Simonetta Giorgi
è la segretaria di direzione

Servizio acquisti
Salvador Perez
è responsabile per il
Servizio acquisti È spagnolo

Servizio Vendite
Tommaso Fiore
coordina le vendite

DIALOGO 1   *Si fa conoscenza*

Michael Moor incontra* il personale della sezione commerciale. (incontrare)

Michael Moor meets some of the Italsistemi personnel in the commercial department.

PRESENTAZIONI

Nome: Matteo
Cognome: Cerulli
Nazionalità:
italiano
Età: 43 anni
Occupazione:
direttore
commerciale
Stato civile: sposato

Nome: Tommaso
Cognome: Fiore
Nazionalità:
italiano
Età: 30 anni
Occupazione:
coordinatore
vendite
Stato civile: celibe

 Studiate queste espressioni, ascoltatele e ripetetele nelle pause previste.

vi presento	*may I introduce . . . to you (lit: I am introducing to you)*
benvenuto	*welcome*
il collega	*the colleague*
non parlo* (parlare)	*I don't speak*
lentamente	*slowly*
al servizio vendite	*in the sales department*
lavora* (lavorare)	*he works*
di dov'è?	*where are you from? (lit: where are you of?)*
studio* (studiare)	*I am studying*
a	*at or in*

Adesso chiudete il libro e ascoltate il dialogo.

SIMONETTA GIORGI:	Vi presento Michael Moor, lo studente inglese.
MATTEO CERULLI:	Piacere, Matteo Cerulli. Benvenuto alla Italsistemi. Questo è il collega, Tommaso Fiore che lavora . . .
MICHAEL MOOR:	Scusi, dottore. Lentamente, per favore. Non parlo molto bene l'italiano.
MATTEO CERULLI:	Questo è Tommaso Fiore. Lavora al servizio vendite.
TOMMASO FIORE:	Piacere, Michael. Di dov'è? Di Londra?
MICHAEL MOOR:	No, sono di Bristol ma studio a Londra.

Ascoltate il dialogo di nuovo, questa volta con il libro aperto. Usate il tasto pausa e ripetete ogni frase.

ESERCIZIO 1.1

Form a group of four and practise the dialogue together, changing roles so that you practise each part in turn. Do this until you feel confident about doing it without the book.

GRAMMATICA

How to say 'the'

We have already seen some ways of saying 'the' in Italian (see p. 11). You need to add another to that list:

Lo   *as in*   lo studente

Lo is used when followed by a masculine noun beginning with the letter 's' plus a consonant or with 'z', or 'ps'.

lo sconto *the discount*   lo zero *the zero*   lo psicologo *the psychologist*

DA NOTARE

il collega *the (male) colleague*
la collega *the (female) colleague*
un collega *a (male) colleague*
una collega *a (female) colleague*

Sono di Bristol means 'I am **of** Bristol' and not '**from** Bristol' when referring to the place where you were born and brought up.

It is customary to use a person's title when addressing them as a sign of respect. To an engineer, you would say *ingegnere*; to an architect, *architetto* etc. Before a name, e.g. *dottor Cerulli*, dottore is shortened to *dottor*. **NB** dottore (masc), *dottoressa* (fem.).

ESERCIZIO 1.2

Vero o falso?

	Vero	Falso

1 Michael Moor non è inglese.
2 Matteo Cerulli parla rapidamente.
3 Tommaso Fiore lavora al servizio acquisti.
4 Matteo Cerulli presenta Tommaso Fiore.
5 Michael Moor è di Londra.

ESERCIZIO 1.3

In each of the following sentences, fill in the gap with the appropriate form of the verb provided.

1 lavorare* *to work*

FRANCO: Sono italiano e .... (lavoro/lavora) per la Olivetti.
MICHAEL: Sono studente. Non .... (lavoro/lavora).
MATTEO: Tommaso .... (lavoro/lavora) al servizio vendite.
MICHAEL: E Lei, Matteo, dove .... (lavoro, lavora)?

2 trovare* *to find*
   Michael non .... (trovo/trova) la chiave.
   Simonetta .... (trovo/trova) Matteo in ufficio.

MICHAEL: .... (Trovo/Trova) l'italiano difficile.
MICHAEL: Tommaso, ... (trovo/trova) il lavoro interessante?

3 accompagnare* *to accompany*
   Simonetta non .... (accompagno/accompagna) Michael in albergo.
   Tommaso .... (accompagno/accompagna) Matteo a Bologna.

4 arrivare* *to arrive*
   Tommaso non .... (arrivo/arriva) con Matteo.
   Simonetta .... (arrivo/arriva) subito.

5 parlare* *to speak*

MICHAEL: Non .... (parlo/parla) molto bene l'italiano.
MATTEO: Michael, Lei è studente. Dove .... (studio/studia)?

6 incontrare* to meet
   Oggi Michael .... (incontro/incontra) il personale della sezione.

ESERCIZIO 1.4

Listen to the numbers 20 to 40 on cassette and repeat them in the pauses provided as many times as you need to learn them.

Can you identify the following numbers in Italian? Listen to the cassette to check your answers

1 24   **2** 17   **3** 38   **4** 7   **5** 21   **6** 43

ESERCIZIO 1.5

Look at p. 24 *Presentazioni*. If Matteo Cerulli were introducing himself, what might he say?

Sono .... Sono .... di nazionalità. Ho .... anni. Sono ....
.... alla Italsistemi. Sono ....

ESERCIZIO 1.6

Now introduce Tommaso Fiore to a colleague using the information on p. 24.

Questo è .... È .... di nazionalità. Ha .... anni. È .... alla
Italsistemi. È ....

ESERCIZIO 1.7

Your supervisor visits you during your work experience. Introduce Matteo Cerulli and Tommaso Fiore to her. Listen to the cassette. The prompts will help you.

ESERCIZIO 1.8

Introduce the following people to your colleagues.

ESERCIZIO 1.9

You are introduced to a Spanish colleague and make polite conversation. Listen to the prompts on the cassette and play your part.

ESERCIZIO 1.10

Match up the sentences in the two columns.

a L'italiano non è . . .	**1** italiano
b Il lavoro è . . .	**2** interessante
c Lo studente è . . .	**3** difficile
d Il collega è . . .	**4** inglese
e Tommaso Fiore è . . .	**5** spagnolo

DIALOGO 2   *Dov'è*

Simonetta Giorgi visita* gli uffici con Michael Moor. (*visitare)

Simonetta Giorgi shows Michael Moor around the offices.

Studiate queste espressioni, ascoltatele sulla cassetta e ripetetele nelle pause previste.

qui	*here*
la sala proiezioni	*the projection room*
dietro	*behind*
la sala riunioni	*the meeting room*
la toeletta	*the toilet*
davanti	*in front*
questa porta	*this door*
certo	*of course*
il servizio acquisti	*the Purchasing Department*
il servizio vendite	*the Sales Department*
mio	*my*
lì in fondo	*down there*
accanto	*next door*

Adesso chiudete il libro e ascoltate il dialogo.

SIMONETTA GIORGI: Allora, qui a destra, c'è la sala proiezioni e . . . dietro c'è la sala riunioni.

MICHAEL MOOR: Questa è la toeletta davanti?

SIMONETTA GIORGI: Sì, questa porta a destra . . . Subito qui a sinistra, c'è il servizio acquisti . . . e dietro . . . il servizio vendite dove lavora Tommaso Fiore.

MICHAEL MOOR: E Lei, dove lavora?

SIMONETTA GIORGI: Il mio ufficio è lì in fondo e accanto, c'è l'ufficio del dottor Cerulli.

Ascoltate il dialogo di nuovo, questa volta con il libro aperto. Usate il tasto pausa e ripetete ogni frase.

ESERCIZIO 2.1

Choose a role and practise the dialogue with a partner. Move on to another partner and practise the same role. When you feel confident that you can do so without the book, change roles. Repeat the process as many times as you need.

ESERCIZIO 2.2

Listen to *Dialogo 2* once again. Are you able to identify the rooms on the plan of the first floor of the Italsistemi building below? There are a few clues to help you.

DA NOTARE

Aldo è **dietro** Michael
Michael è **davanti** a Aldo

Michael è **accanto** a Simonetta

ESERCIZIO 2.3

Michael has his photograph taken with the people he will be working with. Can you answer the questions below?

chi? 'who?'

1 Chi è dietro Michael Moor a sinistra?
2 Chi è accanto a Matteo Cerulli a destra?
3 Chi è accanto a Tommaso Fiore?
4 Chi è davanti a Matteo Cerulli?

ESERCIZIO 2.4

You could bring a group photograph of your own to class and explain who is who in the photograph – in Italian of course!

GRAMMATICA   *Describing people or things*

The words we use to describe people or things are called adjectives. Just like nouns (see p. 11) they have three types of endings in the singular.

Adjectives ending in 'o' are masculine
Adjectives ending in 'a' are feminine
Adjectives ending in 'e' can be either masculine or feminine

In Italian the adjective agrees with the noun it is describing, so you say:

Matteo è simpatic**o**	*Matteo is pleasant*
Simonetta è simpatic**a**	*Simonetta is pleasant*
Matteo è intelligent**e**	*Matteo is intelligent*
Simonetta è intelligent**e**	*Simonetta is intelligent*

Here are some adjectives which you might like to hear describing you:

bravo/brava	*good (e.g. at your job)*
competente	*competent*
bello/bella	*good looking*
giovane	*young*
intelligente	*intelligent*
grande	*big, tall or grown up*
simpatico/simpatica	*nice, pleasant, friendly*
interessante	*interesting*

You will now hear these words on cassette. Repeat them in the pauses provided.

ESERCIZIO 2.5

You overhear some office gossip. You will not understand all of it but listen out for the key words above and see just how much of it you do understand.

What do you learn about
a Simonetta Giorgi?
b Matteo Cerulli?
c Michael Moor?
d Tommaso Fiore?

GRAMMATICA   *il mio, la mia* – my

For 'my', 'your', 'his', 'her' etc. you usually use the equivalent of 'the my', 'the your' etc. and they agree with the noun which follows. See *Grammatica* p. 11.

il mio, la mia	*my*
il **mio** ufficio	*my office*
la **mia** agenda	*my diary*
il suo, la sua	*your, his, her, its*
il **suo** ufficio	*your, his, her office*
la **sua** agenda	*your, his, her diary*

One exception to this is when you are talking about a member of your family in the singular, e.g. *mio fratello* 'my brother', *mia sorella* 'my sister', *mio marito* 'my husband', *mia moglie* 'my wife'.

ESERCIZIO 2.6

Listen to the cassette then answer the following questions.

Modello   Domanda: Questa è la fermata di Michael?
            Risposta: Sì, è la sua fermata.
            o: No, non è la sua fermata.

FERMATA 19

1 Questa è l'agenda di Tommaso?

2 Questa è la camera di Michael?

3 Questa è la chiave di Michael?

4 Questo è l'ufficio di Tommaso?

5 Questo è il passaporto di Matteo?

ESERCIZIO 2.7

Listen to the cassette and ask the questions suggested to you by the prompts.

Modello   Stimolo: *Ask Mr Moor if this is his passport.*
            Lei: Questo è il suo passaporto, signor Moor?

ESERCIZIO 2.8

Fill in the gaps with the words below.

Tommaso Fiore è ...., di Bologna. .... per la Italsistemi al servizio
.... Il .... ufficio è .... l'ufficio della Sezione Acquisti. Tommaso
trova il suo lavoro molto ....

| lavora | suo | italiano | interessante | dietro | vendite |

ESERCIZIO 2.9

Look at *Esercizio 2.8*. Could you write a similar profile for Simonetta Giorgi and Matteo Cerulli?

GRAMMATICA   *Prepositions*

a means 'at' or 'to'; *in* means 'in'; *di* means 'of'; *da* means 'from'; *su* means 'on': but you will only find them in these forms when they are followed by the name of a person or a place and in a few set expressions, e.g. *in albergo*. This is because they change when used in conjunction with the words for 'the'.

	il	lo	l'	la
a	al	allo	all'	alla
in	nel	nello	nell'	nella
di	del	dello	dell'	della
da	dal	dallo	dall'	dalla
su	sul	sullo	sull'	sulla

ESERCIZIO 2.10

Listen to the cassette and fill in the gaps in the exercise below. Can you say where the following items are to be found?

1 La cassetta è accanto .... telefono.
2 L'indirizzo di Tommaso è .... 'agenda.
3 Il passaporto di Michael è .... tavola.
4 La chiave .... sua camera è .... ricezione?
5 Salvador arriva .... Madrid oggi.

DIALOGO 3   *Che cosa fa?*

Michael Moor s'informa* sul lavoro della sezione. (*informarsi)

Michael Moor finds out about the work of the department.

Studiate queste espressioni, ascoltatele e ripetetele nelle pause previste.

non capisco* (capire)	*I don't understand*
cosa fa?* (fare)	*what does he/she do?*
responsabile	*responsible*
tutta la sezione	*the whole section*
coordina* (coordinare)	*coordinates*
le operazioni di vendita	*the sales operations*
ecco!	*here is!*
guardi!* (guardare)	*look!*
ho capito	*I have understood*
esatto	*exactly*

Adesso chiudete il libro e ascoltate il dialogo.

MICHAEL MOOR: Scusi, non capisco bene. Che cosa fa il dottor Cerulli?
SIMONETTA GIORGI: È il direttore commerciale. È responsabile per tutta la sezione, acquisti e vendite.
MICHAEL MOOR: E Tommaso Fiore, allora?
SIMONETTA GIORGI: Tommaso coordina tutte le operazioni di vendita. Ecco una scheda! Guardi!
MICHAEL MOOR: Ho capito. E Lei è la segretaria del dottor Cerulli, vero?
SIMONETTA GIORGI: Esatto.

Ascoltate il dialogo di nuovo, questa volta con il libro aperto. Usate il tasto pausa e ripetete ogni frase.

ESERCIZIO 3.1

Choose a role and practise the dialogue with a partner. Move on to another partner and practise the same role. When you feel sure of it, change roles. Repeat the process as many times as you need.

GRAMMATICA   *Capire** – to understand

The verb 'understand' is listed under *capire* in the dictionary. Many (but not all) of the verbs ending in *ire* will follow this pattern.

Capire
capisco	*I understand*
capisce	*you understand*
	he/she/it understands
finire	*finish*
reagire	*react*
gestire	*manage a company/affairs*
fornire	*supply*

DA NOTARE

*Fare** – to do or to make

Che cosa fa? Some verbs have very irregular forms. *Fa* comes from the verb *fare* 'do' or 'make'.

faccio   *I do/I am doing, I make/I am making*
fa   *you do/you are doing, you make/you are making, he/she/it does/is doing, he/she/it makes/is making*

ESERCIZIO 3.2

Vero o falso?

	Vero	**Falso**
1 Michael Moor non capisce bene.		
2 Il dottor Cerulli coordina tutte le operazioni di vendita.		
3 Tommaso Fiore è responsabile per tutta la sezione.		
4 Simonetta Giorgi è la segretaria di Matteo Cerulli.		

ESERCIZIO 3.3

Look at the diagram below explaining the kind of work the sales office deals with. Now read the statements below and rearrange them in the correct order.

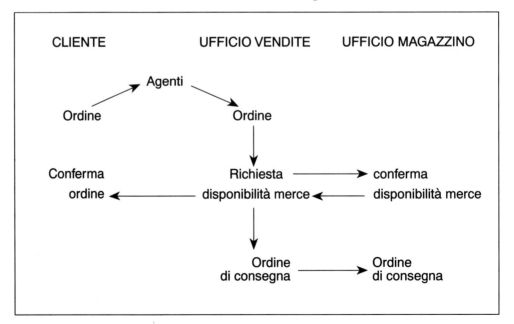

1 L'ufficio vendite conferma l'ordine al cliente.
2 L'ufficio vendite fa una richiesta di disponibilità merce all'ufficio magazzino.
3 Il cliente manda l'ordine all'ufficio vendite.
4 L'ufficio magazzino conferma la disponibilità merce all'ufficio vendite.
5 L'ufficio vendite manda un ordine di consegna all'ufficio magazzino.

ESERCIZIO 3.4

If you found yourself in the following situations, which form of the verb would you use?

1 Simonetta is explaining something to you and you do not understand.
Non .... (capisco *or* capisce?)
2 You need to check that Tommaso finishes work at six.
E Lei, signor Fiore .... il lavoro alle sei, vero?   (finisco *or* finisce?)
3 You are explaining to someone that Doctor Cerulli manages the whole of the section.
Il dottor Cerulli .... tutta la sezione.   (gestisco *or* gestisce?)
4 You think that you are reacting well in this situation.
.... bene in questa situazione.   (reagisco *or* reagisce?)
5 Tommaso calls you into his office but you have to finish this before you go.
Un attimo, per piacere. .... questo e arrivo subito.   (finisco *or* finisce?)

GRAMMATICA   *Plurals*

You have already seen nouns in the singular p. 11. Now you need to know the plural forms.

	singular		plural endings
masculine nouns ending in:	o	→	i
feminine nouns ending in:	a	→	e
masculine nouns ending in:	e	→	i
feminine nouns ending in:	e	→	i

Similarly the word for 'the' changes in the plural:

	singular	plural
masculine	il documento	i documenti
	lo studente	gli studenti
	l'albergo	gli alberghi
feminine	la scheda	le schede
	l'operazione	le operazioni

ESERCIZIO 3.5

Can you work out what the plurals of the following words would be?

1 il passaporto
2 l'ufficio
3 lo studio
4 il portiere
5 lo studente
6 la signora
7 la chiave
8 l'edicola
9 il libro
10 l'aeroporto
11 lo scenario
12 il dottore
13 lo scozzese
14 la fermata
15 la situazione
16 l'automobile
17 il centro
18 l'albergo
19 la porta

DA NOTARE   *How to say 'all'*

To say 'all' or 'the whole', use the appropriate form of *tutto* together with the correct form of 'the'.

tutto il processo	*the whole process*
tutta la sezione	*the whole section*
tutti i documenti	*all the documents*
tutte le operazioni	*all the operations*

ESERCIZIO 3.6

Which form of *tutto* would you use in the following phrases? Check with *Grammatica* on p. 37 that you know how to say 'the' in each case. What do they all mean?

1 .... sezione
2 .... giorno
3 .... uffici
4 .... agende
5 .... sera
6 .... colleghi

ESERCIZIO 3.7

Which form would you use in the following sentences: *faccio* or *fa*?

1 Simonetta Giorgi .... bene il suo lavoro.
2 Sono inglese e .... tirocinio in Italia.
3 Tommaso Fiore .... una richiesta all'ufficio magazzino.
4 E Lei, cosa .... a Bologna?

ESERCIZIO 3.8

Listen to the cassette and answer the following questions.

1 Where is Rebecca Powell and what is she doing there?
2 How has she got to know Marisa Marinelli?
3 How old is Marisa?
4 Is she married?
5 What is she like as a person?
6 What work does she do?
7 Is she very busy?
8 What languages does she speak?

ESERCIZIO 3.9

For this exercise, the class will be divided into A and B students. The student A role is to be found on this page. The student B role is to be found on p. 46.

Student A

You work for the Olivetti company in the sales office. A student has been assigned to do work experience in your office. When s/he arrives s/he will explain why s/he has come. You will need to ask a few questions and be prepared to answer questions that are put to you.

Study your role for a few moments and decide what you are going to say about yourself and what questions you are going to ask the other person.

Hello, pleased to meet you

Are you Italian?

Where do you come from?

Is everything OK?

I work in the sales department

I coordinate sales operations

I find the work very interesting

DIALOGO 4 · *Una pausa meritata*

BAR

Simonetta e Michael fanno* una pausa con Tommaso. (*fare)

Simonetta and Michael take a break with Tommaso.

Studiate queste espressioni, ascoltatele e ripetetele nelle pause previste.

prendiamo?* (prendere)	*shall we have? (lit: shall we take?)*
volentieri	*willingly*
vieni* anche tu? (venire)	*are you coming too?*
preferisce?, preferisci?* (preferire)	*do you prefer?*
diamoci del tu!	*let's be less formal! (lit: let's call each other 'tu')*

 Adesso chiudete il libro e ascoltate il dialogo.

SIMONETTA GIORGI: Prendiamo un caffè?
MICHAEL MOOR: Volentieri.
SIMONETTA GIORGI: Vieni anche tu, Tommaso?
TOMMASO FIORE: Sì, arrivo subito.
SIMONETTA GIORGI: Michael, cosa preferisce? . . . ma no . . . diamoci del tu! . . . cosa preferisci?
MICHAEL MOOR: Un cappuccino, grazie.
TOMMASO FIORE: E per me un espresso.
SIMONETTA GIORGI: Va bene. Un cappuccino e due espressi.

 Ascoltate il dialogo di nuovo, questa volta con il libro aperto. Usate il tasto pausa e ripetete ogni frase.

ESERCIZIO 4.1

Form a group of three and practise the dialogue together, changing roles so that you practise each part in turn.

GRAMMATICA   *Formal or informal?*

In Italian, we have a choice between addressing people formally or informally. Not only are there different words for 'you', *Lei* being formal and *tu* informal, but the form of the verb changes, too.

Formal	Informal	
Lei preferisc**e**?	**Tu** preferisc**i**?	*Do you prefer?*
A che ora arriv**a**?	A che ora arriv**i**?	*At what time are you arriving?*
Che cosa prend**e**?	Che cosa prend**i**?	*What are you having?*

NB If the verb ends in 'i' then the informal form is being used.

Use *Lei* when addressing a superior in a company or someone you have just met or as a term of respect for someone older.

Use *tu* once you have established a friendship with someone or with a peer or with a young person.

Notice in *Dialogo 4* that Simonetta says to Michael: *diamoci del tu* that is, 'let's call each other *tu*'. In other words, 'we are on friendly terms now'.

ESERCIZIO 4.2

On the cassette you will hear snippets of conversations. Decide whether the person speaking is addressing a friend or a superior.

	1	2	3	4	5	6	7	8
Friend								
Superior								

DA NOTARE

Some verbs do not follow any set pattern and have to be learnt:

venire   *to come*
vengo   *I come, I am coming*
vieni   *you come, you are coming (informal)*
viene   *you come, you are coming (formal)*
viene   *he, she, it comes or is coming*

essere *to be*	avere *to have*	fare *to do, make*	
sono	ho	faccio	*l*
sei	hai	fai	*you (informal)*
è	ha	fa	*you (formal)*
è	ha	fa	*he she, it*

ESERCIZIO 4.3

You wish to ask the same questions of Simonetta and Tommaso but now that Simonetta is a friend, you will address her informally. What will you say?

1 vieni?
  viene?   .... al bar?   .... al bar?
2 prende?
  prendi?   .... un caffè?   .... un caffè?
3 lavori?   .... molto in questo   .... molto in questo
  lavora?   momento?   momento?
4 è?
  sei?   .... stanca?   .... stanco?
5 hai?
  ha?   .... famiglia?   .... famiglia?

ESERCIZIO 4.4

This conversation is jumbled up. Can you put it in the right order?

1
> Bene, grazie

2
> Sì, volentieri

3
> Cosa prendi, un caffè?

4
> Ciao Sergio

5
> Com'è andato il vaggio

6
> Andiamo al bar

7
> D'accordo

DA NOTARE   – *iamo*

If you hear *iamo* at the end of a verb, you know that it means either 'we' or 'let's' e.g. *prendiamo un caffè* 'let's have (lit. take) a coffee', *andiamo al bar* 'let's go to the bar'.

ESERCIZIO 4.5

These captions are all taken from the business journals *Mondo Economico* and *il Mondo*. Can you deduce what they are about? If you are unsure, use the glossary at the back of the book.

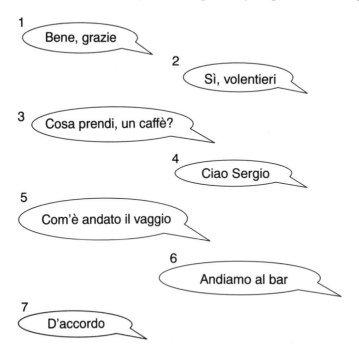

1 Benvenuti a Washington.
Anzi, Aloha.

ESERCIZIO 4.6

Simonetta is thinking about a holiday and is looking at a holiday brochure. Can you decide what kinds of holidays this firm specialises in? Perhaps you could rewrite the captions in English?

PER TUTTI

COPPIE

SINGLE

FAMIGLIA

SPOSI

RAGAZZI

NB You may use the following three exercises in two ways. Either in class with a partner or a group where you will alternate roles or by listening to the cassette and interacting with the speakers.

ESERCIZIO 4.7

You will take the part of Michael Moor. You have the opportunity to visit the Ferrari factory at Maranello, Modena. You invite Simonetta to go with you. On arrival, you decide to do all the talking. You have been told that a Dr Sampino will show you round. The prompts will help you decide what to say.

PORTIERE: Buongiorno, desidera?
LEI: *Good morning, I am Michael Moor and this is my colleague Simonetta Giorgi. Is Dr Sampino there, please?*
PORTIERE: Un attimo. Ah, dottor Sampino, ci sono due persone che l'aspettano in ricezione . . . il signor Michael Moor e la signorina Simonetta Giorgi . . . Va bene . . . Arriva subito.
SAMPINO: Buongiorno, Augusto Sampino, piacere.
LEI: *Michael Moor, I'm pleased to meet you. This is Simonetta Giorgi.*
SAMPINO: Piacere, signorina.

ESERCIZIO 4.8

The visit at the Ferrari factory continues: carry on the conversation:

SAMPINO: Lei è inglese, vero?
LEI: *Yes I am from Bristol and I am studying in London.*
SAMPINO: E che cosa fa qui in Italia?
LEI: *I am doing work experience at the Italsistemi.*
SAMPINO: Ma parla bene l'italiano
LEI: *Oh, not very well. And what do **you** do?*
SAMPINO: Sono direttore delle vendite in Italia.

ESERCIZIO 4.9

The visit at the Ferrari factory continues. Dr Sampino shows Michael and Simonetta the production line. Continue the conversation.

SAMPINO: Qui a sinistra abbiamo l'ufficio magazzino. Entriamo.
LEI: *It's very large. Who is responsible for this section?*
SAMPINO: Il direttore di produzione ma non è qui in questo momento. Andiamo a vedere la nuova Testarossa . . .
LEI: *And this is the new Testarossa?*
SAMPINO: Sì la nuova . . . è bella, vero?
LEI: *Oh yes, it is very beautiful.*

Prima di continuare

Before going on to the next chapter, make sure that you know how to:

• engage in small talk	*di dov'è* *sono di Bristol* *ha famiglia?*
• ask what people do	*che lavoro fa?* *coordina le operazioni vendite?*
• say you do not understand	*non capisco bene*
• ask for clarification	*che cosa fa?*
• address people formally	*cosa preferisce?*
• or informally	*vieni anche tu?*
• use official titles	*scusi, dottore*
• describe people and things	*è simpatico* *è difficile*
• state precisely where things are located	*accanto a/dietro*

ESERCIZIO 3.9

Student B role for *Esercizio 3.9* on p. 39.

You are a British student from Coventry. You are on work experience at the Olivetti company and everything seems to be going well at the moment. You have been assigned to work with Student A. Go to the reception to meet her/him and explain why you have come. Try to find out something about your partner.

Study your role for a few moments and decide what you are going to say about yourself and what questions you are going to ask the other person.

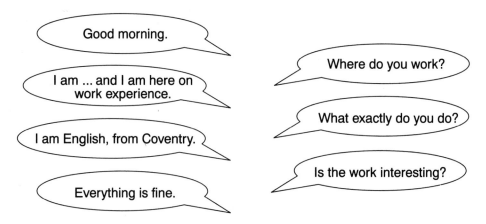

La giornata lavorativa

THE WORKING DAY

> **In this chapter you will talk about:**
> * office routine
> * precise time
> * what exactly people do
> * what you are interested in doing

DIALOGO 1 *A che ora?*

BAR

Simonetta torna* con le bibite. (*tornare)

Simonetta returns with the drinks.

📼 Studiate queste espressioni, ascoltatele e ripetetele nelle pause previste.

a che ora?	at what time?
cominciate?* (cominciare)	do you begin?
la mattina	(in) the morning
finite?* (finire)	do you finish?
la sera	(in) the evening
davvero?	really?
una giornata	a day
con tre pause	with three breaks
mezzogiorno	midday
pomeriggio	afternoon

📼 Adesso chiudete il libro e ascoltate il dialogo.

MICHAEL MOOR:	A che ora cominciate la mattina?
TOMMASO FIORE:	Alle otto.
MICHAEL MOOR:	Alle otto? E a che ora finite la sera?
TOMMASO FIORE:	Finiamo alle diciotto e trenta.
MICHAEL MOOR:	Davvero. È una giornata molto lunga.
SIMONETTA GIORGI:	Sì, è lunga – otto ore di lavoro con tre pause, mattina, mezzogiorno e pomeriggio.

📼 Ascoltate il dialogo di nuovo, questa volta con il libro aperto. Usate il tasto pausa e ripetete ogni frase.

ESERCIZIO 1.1

Form a group of three and practise the dialogue together, changing roles so that you practise each part in turn. Do this as many times as you need. It is quite a useful exercise to record yourselves and compare your recording with the original cassette.

GRAMMATICA *Speaking to two or more people*

When speaking to two or more people you use a different form of the verb:

cominci**ate**	*you begin*
fin**ite**	*you finish*

For verbs ending in *are* e.g. *cominciare* take off *are* and add *ate*: cominciate.
For those ending in *ere* e.g. *prendere* take off *ere* and add *ete*: prendete.
For those ending in *ire* e.g. *finire* take off *ire* and add *ite*: finite.

DA NOTARE *Irregular verbs*

Some verbs do not follow a set pattern:

essere *to be* → siete *you are*

ESERCIZIO 1.2

Listen to the cassette and decide if the person speaking in each case is addressing one person, or more than one, and tick the columns accordingly. Then listen to the cassette again and where you have decided that only one person is being addressed, consider whether that person is a friend or an acquaintance (see p. 40) and tick the remaining columns.

	one person	more than one person	formally	informally
1				
2				
3				
4				
5				
6				

ESERCIZIO 1.3

You are talking to Simonetta and Tommaso about their work. Which form of the verb in brackets would you use in the following sentences?

1 A che ora .... (arrivare) in ufficio?
2 .... (prendere) un caffè o .... (cominciare) subito a lavorare?
3 A che ora .... (fare) la pausa la mattina? .... (mangiare) alla mensa o .... (andare) fuori al ristorante?
4 A che ora .... (finire) il lavoro la sera?

GRAMMATICA

How to say 'we'

When you wish to say 'we', you take off the endings in the same way as for 'you' plural and you add *iamo* to all forms, e.g. *finiamo, prendiamo*.

For verbs ending in *are* e.g. *parlare* take off *are* and add *iamo*: parliamo.
For verbs ending in *ere* e.g. *prendere* take off *ere* and add *iamo*: prendiamo.
For verbs ending in *ire* e.g. *finire* take off *ire* and add *iamo*: finiamo.
For *cominciamo*, (cominciare) however, you just add *amo* because there is already an 'i'.

DA NOTARE

More irregular verbs

avere	*to have*	→	abbiamo	*we have*
essere	*to be*	→	siamo	*we are*
fare	*to do, make*	→	facciamo	*we do, make*

ESERCIZIO 1.4

A colleague is writing a short account of how your department functions. She is checking that she has her facts right. She has been very thorough in her research so all you have to do is to confirm what she says, using the 'we' form.

Modello   Domanda: Voi cominciate il lavoro alle 8.00 di mattina, vero?
              Risposta: Sì, cominciamo alle otto.

ESERCIZIO 1.5

Listen to the numbers 50 to 70 on cassette and repeat them in the pauses provided as many times as you need to learn them.

How would you say the following numbers in Italian?

1 40   **2** 45   **3** 50   **4** 55   **5** 60   **6** 70

Listen to the cassette to check your answers.

DA NOTARE

The 24-hour clock

Italians normally use the 24-hour clock for anything official, so it will be the most useful one to learn.

A CHE ORA . . . . ?

mattina o pomeriggio

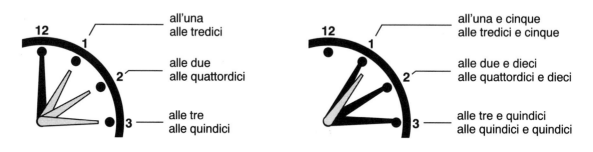

To ask at what time something is happening, use *a che ora?* literally, 'at what hour?'

A che ora cominciamo la mattina?

The answer will usually be *alle* plus the time:

alle otto   *at eight*

except for 'at one o'clock' which is *all'una*.

When you need to say 'from . . . to', use *'dalle . . . alle'*.

dalle quattordici alle sedici   *from two to four in the afternoon.*

ESERCIZIO 1.6

Listen to the schedule planned for this half-day conference. Make a note of the times.

24-hour clock

RISTORANTE

Start time	
Finish	
Break from	
to	
Film begins at	
Finishes at	
Dinner	

ESERCIZIO 1.7

lunedì	**_31 Marzo_**
08.00	lavoro
10.00 - 10.15	pausa per il caffè
12.30 - 14.30	pausa per il pranzo
14.30	lavoro
16.00 - 16.15	pausa
16.15	lavoro
18.30	fine della giornata lavorativa

Look at the schedule above. What would Simonetta and Tommaso's answers be to the questions in *Esercizio 1.3*? They always start work straight away in the morning, and they do not take coffee. At lunchtime they prefer not to eat in the *mensa*, the office canteen, but to go out to a restaurant.

ESERCIZIO 1.8

1 What would you be looking for if you went to the *Borsa immobiliare di Milano*?
2 Where is it?
3 Is it far away?

ESERCIZIO 1.9

CERCHIAMO CLIENTI ESIGENTI

Siamo una società che gestisce una vasta gamma di servizi collegati al trasporto e alla distribuzione per i più importanti istituti di credito, assicurativi e finanziari.
Da oltre vent'anni.
Non offriamo un semplice servizio di corriere nazionale e internazionale.
Studiamo e realizziamo "il servizio" che Voi volete: con le modalità, i tempi, e i mezzi necessari a soddisfare le vostre richieste.
Siamo l'unico corriere nazionale che gestisce una flotta di aerei di proprietà per i collegamenti più urgenti.

In this advertisement, CISES informs the reader what they do. *Cerchiamo* means 'we are looking for'. How many other references can you find to what 'we' do in the passage?

You will probably be able to understand the whole passage with the help of the vocabulary below.

una gamma	*a range*
collegati a	*connected with*
più	*more, most*
istituti	*institutions*
assicurativi	*insurance*
oltre	*over*
servizio di corriere	*postal service*
le modalità	*formalities*
i tempi	*the times*
i mezzi	*the means*
soddisfare	*satisfy*
le vostre richieste	*your requests*
i collegamenti	*connections*
di proprietà	*of its own*

DIALOGO 2   *Al servizio vendite*

Michael va* al servizio vendite dove osserva* Tommaso Fiore. (*andare, *osservare)

Michael goes to the Sales Department where he will observe Tommaso Fiore.

Studiate queste espressioni, ascoltatele e ripetetele nelle pause previste.

che lavoro fa?	what work do you do?
sono spesso in contatto	I am often in contact
con gli agenti	with the agents
quanti?	how many?
anche	also
tre filiali	three branches
quindi	so
Lei viaggia* molto? (viaggiare)	do you travel a lot?
abbastanza	quite a lot
almeno	at least
una volta al mese	once a month

Adesso chiudete il libro e ascoltate il dialogo.

MICHAEL MOOR: Tommaso, Lei, che lavoro fa esattamente?
TOMMASO FIORE: Io coordino le operazioni vendite e sono spesso in contatto con gli agenti.
MICHAEL MOOR: Quanti agenti di vendita ci sono?
TOMMASO FIORE: Diciannove in tutta l'Italia. Abbiamo anche tre filiali.
MICHAEL MOOR: Davvero? Dove?
TOMMASO FIORE: A Bari, a Brescia e a Roma.
MICHAEL MOOR: Quindi, Lei viaggia molto?
TOMMASO FIORE: Abbastanza. Visito le filiali almeno una volta al mese.

Ascoltate il dialogo di nuovo, questa volta con il libro aperto. Usate il tasto pausa e ripetete ogni frase.

ESERCIZIO 2.1

Practise the dialogue with a partner making sure your pronunciation is correct. Retaining the same role, move to another partner and practise again. When you are sure you can do this without the book, change roles and repeat the process.

DA NOTARE

Io means 'I' and as we have seen it is not strictly necessary in Italian to indicate who is doing the action of the verb. As with *Lei* meaning 'you', it is usually used for emphasis.

In this dialogue, you have learnt several useful words which though not absolutely essential to basic understanding, help the flow of the conversation: *esattamente, spesso, quindi, abbastanza, almeno, davvero.*

Add these to the one-liners you have learnt previously: *certo, allora, volentieri, subito, prego, va bene, un attimo, lentamente, per favore.*

ESERCIZIO 2.2

When you are learning a foreign language it is always useful to be able to say a lot in few words. Which of the following short answers would you give in the situations suggested on cassette?

> davvero

> sì, subito

> esattamente

> lentamente, per favore

> volentieri

> certo

Modello   Domanda: Lei è qui per fare tirocinio, se capisco bene?
              Stimolo: *Confirm that that's exactly why you are here.*
              Risposta: Esattamente.

ESERCIZIO 2.3

Vero o falso? Look back at the dialogue and decide whether the following statements are true or false.

	Vero	Falso
1 Tommaso è spesso in contatto con gli agenti.		
2 Ci sono diciotto agenti di vendita.		
3 Le tre filiali non sono in Italia.		
4 Tommaso non viaggia molto.		
5 Tommaso visita la famiglia una volta al mese.		

ESERCIZIO 2.4

Listen to the names of some Italian towns. Can you fill in the names on the map? Have a competition with a partner to see who is the most accurate.

DA NOTARE   *Quanto*

Quante volte hai desiderato
di avere le ali ai piedi?

QUANTE RAGIONI IN PIÙ PER DIRE FRAU!

Quanti sorrisi persi per le macchie sui denti.

DENIVIT. LA RIVINCITA DEL SORRISO.

Quanta poesia c'è nella tua vita?

PARKER SONNET

When used on its own, *quanto* may mean 'how much?', 'how long?', 'how far?' etc. depending on the verb which follows it.

quanto costa?	*how much does it cost?*
quanto dura?	*how long does it last?*
quanto dista da Bologna?	*how far is it from Bologna?*

But when *quanto* is used with a noun, it means 'how much?' or 'how many?'. Note how the form changes:

(il denaro)
↓
quanto denaro?

(i documenti)
↓
quanti documenti?

(la memoria)
↓
quanta memoria?

(le persone)
↓
quante persone?

ESERCIZIO 2.5

Which of the forms of *quanto* would you use in the questions below: *quanto, quanti, quanta* or *quante*?

1 .... biglietti avete per il cinema?
2 .... camere ci sono in questo hotel?
3 .... memoria ha questo computer?
4 .... ordini ci sono?
5 .... lavoro abbiamo oggi?
6 .... tempo abbiamo per il caffè?
7 .... persone ci sono in questo ufficio?
8 .... dura la classe?
9 .... costa il biglietto?

ESERCIZIO 2.6

You are sent to the personnel office to observe Luisa Polo. You still feel very new, so you need to ask a lot of questions to understand things better. Below, you will find a series of possible questions. The prompts on cassette will help you decide when to use them.

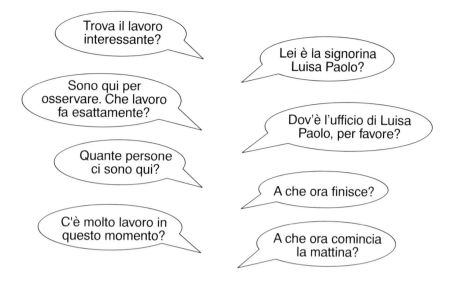

Now listen to the exercise again and try it without looking at the book.

ESERCIZIO 2.7

1 Quanto dista Parma da Bologna?

Parma	←97 km→	Bologna
Ferrara	←47 km→	Bologna
Modena	←51 km→	Bologna

DA	A	VOLO	PARTENZA	ARRIVO	FREQUENZA
MILANO	ROMA	IG1102	7.35	8.40	1234567
MILANO	ROMA	IG1108	8.30	9.35	12345
MILANO	ROMA	IG1104	13.30	14.35	123456
MILANO	ROMA	IG1106	18.30	19.35	123457

2 Quanto dura il viaggio da Milano a Roma in aereo?
3 Quanti voli ci sono al giorno da Milano a Roma?
4 Quanto costa il traduttore?
5 Quante lingue traduce?

6 Make up five further questions of your own based on the illustrations above.

DIALOGO 3 *Che cosa faccio?*

Michael Moor s'informa sul tipo di lavoro che farà.

Michael Moor finds out what type of work he will be doing.

 Studiate queste espressioni, ascoltatele e ripetetele nelle pause previste.

domani	*tomorrow*
Lei sta* con me (stare)	*you stay with me*
come funziona* il servizio (funzionare)	*how the department works*
sarò fuori sede	*I'll be off site*
Lei può* (potere)	*you can*
se vuole* (volere)	*if you wish*
lo conosce*? (conoscere)	*do you know it?*
è molto simile	*it is very similar*

 Adesso chiudete il libro e ascoltate il dialogo.

TOMMASO FIORE: Oggi e domani, Lei sta con me in ufficio per osservare come funziona il servizio.

MICHAEL MOOR: Va bene.

TOMMASO FIORE: E mercoledì io sarò fuori sede e Lei può lavorare al computer, se vuole.

MICHAEL MOOR: Che tipo di computer è?

TOMMASO FIORE: È un Olivetti. Lo conosce?

MICHAEL MOOR: No, io uso un Apple Mac.

TOMMASO FIORE: Un Macintosh? Non è un problema. È molto simile. Ha il programma Windows.

 Ascoltate il dialogo di nuovo, questa volta con il libro aperto. Usate il tasto pausa e ripetete ogni frase.

ESERCIZIO 3.1

Practise the dialogue with a partner, making sure your pronunciation is correct. Retaining the same role, move to another partner and practise again. When you are sure you can do this without the book, change roles and repeat the process.

ESERCIZIO 3.2

Listen to the days of the week on cassette and repeat them in the pauses provided. Do this as many times as necessary in order to learn them.

I giorni della settimana:

lunedì	martedì	mercoledì	giovedì
venerdì	sabato	domenica	

ESERCIZIO 3.3

Vero o falso? Tick the statements which are correct.

	Vero	**Falso**
1 Tommaso Fiore lavora in ufficio martedì e mercoledì.		
2 Tommaso Fiore non lavora in ufficio lunedì.		
3 Michael Moor non usa un Olivetti.		
4 Non è un problema perché l'Apple Mac è molto simile.		

ESERCIZIO 3.4

	lunedì	martedì	mercoledì	giovedì	venerdì	sabato	domenica
mattina							
pomeriggio							
sera							

Listen to the statements on cassette to find out what Matteo Cerulli's engagements are this week. Then fill in the week planner above in Italian.

ESERCIZIO 3.5

Match up the questions and answers in the columns below.

1 Con chi lavora Michael Moor oggi?   a Osserva come funziona la sezione.
2 Che cosa fa?   b Fuori sede.
3 Dove sarà Tommaso mercoledì?   c No, perché è molto simile.
4 Che tipo di computer c'è in ufficio? d Un Olivetti.
5 Michael conosce questo tipo di   e Lavora con Tommaso.
  computer?   f No, di solito usa un Apple Mac.
6 Secondo Tommaso, è un problema?

GRAMMATICA   *Lo* and *la*

Lo can mean 'it' (masculine) or 'him'.
In the dialogue, *lo conosce?* means, 'Do you know **it**?' (lit. it do you know?)
Lo refers to the computer which is masculine.
*Michael? **Lo** conosco bene*, means, 'Michael? I know **him** well'.

La can mean 'it' (feminine) or 'her'.
*Conosce l'Italia? No, non **la** conosco bene*, means 'Do you know Italy?' 'No I don't
know **it** well'. (*La* refers to Italia which is feminine.)
*Simonetta? **La** conosco bene* means, 'Simonetta? I know **her** well.'

ESERCIZIO 3.6

In the following replies to Simonetta's questions, which would Michael use: *lo*
or *la*?

1 Conosci Luisa Paolo?
  Sì, ... conosco un po'.
2 Quando visiti la ditta con Matteo?
  .... visito domani.
3 Capisci questo?
  No, non .... capisco bene.
4 Preferisci il tè con o senza latte?
  .... preferisco con latte.
5 Trovi il lavoro interessante?
  Sì .... trovo molto interessante.

DA NOTARE *Conoscere* – to know or to be acquainted with

This time the words for 'I', 'you' etc. are given in brackets:

(io) conosco	*I know*
(tu) conosci	*you (informal) know*
(Lei) conosce	*you (formal) know*
(lui) conosce	*he knows*
(lei) conosce	*she knows*
(noi) conosciamo	*we know*
(voi) conoscete	*you (plural) know*
(loro) conoscono	*they know*

ESERCIZIO 3.7

Fill in the correct form of *conoscere* in the following dialogue.

Simonetta, Michael and Tommaso are chatting together:

> SIMONETTA: Mike .... l'Italia?
> MICHAEL: No, non la .... bene. E tu, ... l'Inghilterra?
> SIMONETTA: No, ma Tommaso la ....
> TOMMASO: Sì, io .... bene Londra.
> SIMONETTA: Noi andiamo spesso in Irlanda e .... Dublino.
> MICHAEL: Ah, ... Dublino? Anch'io .... Dublino.

GRAMMATICA *More irregular verbs*

Here are some more verbs which do not follow a set pattern:

potere *to be able*	volere *to want to*	
posso	voglio	*I*
puoi	vuoi	*you (informal)*
può	vuole	*you (formal)*
può	vuole	*he, she or it*
possiamo	vogliamo	*we*
potete	volete	*you (plural)*
possono	vogliono	*they*

Posso cambiare del denaro?
Can I change some money, please?

Banca

Posso telefonare in Inghilterra, per piacere?
Can (may) I phone England, please?

Telefono

Vuoi andare al cinema stasera?
Do you want to go to the cinema this evening?

Cinema

Vuoi una penna?
Do you want a pen?

Penna

ESERCIZIO 3.8

Look at the conversation between Tommaso and Simonetta and decide which part of *potere* or *volere* you would use in the blanks.

TOMMASO: ……… andare al cinema stasera? C'è un buon film.
SIMONETTA: Mi dispiace ma non ……… stasera. Mio fratello arriva da Roma. Andiamo al ristorante. ……… venire anche tu?
TOMMASO: Sì, volentieri, grazie.
SIMONETTA: E ……… andare al cinema insieme venerdì, se ……… .
TOMMASO: Va bene. ……… venire anche tuo fratello.
SIMONETTA: No, non ……… . Torna a Roma venerdì mattina.

ESERCIZIO 3.9

There are few differences between different computer edit menus. Join the corresponding commands with a pencil.

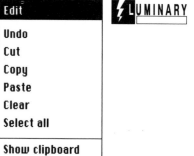

MAXIM · Modifica	Edit · LUMINARY
Annulla	Undo
Taglia	Cut
Copia	Copy
Incolla	Paste
Cancella	Clear
Seleziona tutto	Select all
Ora/data	Show clipboard
A capo automatico	

DIALOGO 4 · *Dove andiamo?*

Michael e Tommaso completano* il programma per la settimana. (*completare)

Michael and Tommaso complete the plan for the week.

 Studiate queste espressioni, ascoltatele e ripetetele nelle pause previste.

il ragioniere	*the accountant*
lontano	*far*
non troppo	*not too*
circa	*about*
dunque	*therefore*
un'ora e mezza	*one and a half hours*
senz'altro	*of course, without a doubt*
Le interessa vedere?	*are you interested in seeing? (lit: is it interesting to you to see?)*
la nostra linea di produzione	*our production line*

 Adesso chiudete il libro e ascoltate il dialogo.

MICHAEL MOOR: E giovedì, cosa facciamo?

TOMMASO FIORE: Visitiamo la filiale di Brescia. Ho un appuntamento con il ragioniere Alessi.

MICHAEL MOOR: È lontano?

TOMMASO FIORE: Non troppo. È a circa 180 chilometri ... dunque un'ora e mezza di macchina.

MICHAEL MOOR: E torniamo a Bologna la sera?

TOMMASO FIORE: Senz'altro ... E per venerdì ... vediamo ... Le interessa vedere la nostra linea di produzione?

MICHAEL MOOR: Certo. Mi interessa molto.

Ascoltate il dialogo di nuovo, questa volta con il libro aperto. Usate il tasto pausa e ripetete ogni frase.

ESERCIZIO 4.1

Practise the dialogue with a partner making sure your pronunciation is correct. Retaining the same role, move to another partner and practise again. When you are sure you can do this without the book, change roles and repeat the process.

GRAMMATICA *To me, to you*

Le and *ti* mean, 'to you'; *mi* means, 'to me'.
Le interessa? literally means, 'is it interesting to you?' when being formal.
You use *ti interessa?* when being informal.
Mi interessa literally means, 'it is interesting to me'.
Non mi interessa means, 'it is not interesting to me'.

ESERCIZIO 4.2

Which would you use in the following exchanges: *Le interessa, ti interessa, mi interessa* or *non mi interessa . . .* ?

TOMMASO FIORE:	.... visitare Firenze?
MICHAEL MOOR:	Sì .... molto.
SIMONETTA GIORGI:	.... vedere un film?
MICHAEL MOOR:	No, ... perché non capisco molto bene l'italiano.
SIMONETTA GIORGI:	.... visitare la ditta?
MICHAEL MOOR:	Sì .... molto.
TOMMASO FIORE:	C'è una conferenza questo pomeriggio, ...?
MICHAEL MOOR:	Mi dispiace ma no, ... vado in città con Simonetta.

ESERCIZIO 4.3

Work with a partner and make up your own conversations following the pattern shown and using the chart below.

Modello	Domanda:	Parma è lontano da Bologna?
	Risposta:	No, non tanto. *(not so far)*
		Abbastanza. *(quite far)*
		Sì molto. *(yes very far)*
	Domanda:	A quanti chilometri?
	Risposta:	A 97 chilometri.

Distanze in chilometri

	Bologna	Firenze	Roma
Bologna	—	104	379
Brescia	179	277	552
Firenze	104	—	271
Genova	273	265	526
Milano	211	299	574
Palermo	1368	1260	994
Parma	97	185	460
Roma	379	271	—
Venezia	160	264	517

ESERCIZIO 4.4

Look at the timetable and answer the questions on cassette.

DA	A	VOLO	PARTENZA	ARRIVO	FREQUENZA
MILANO	ROMA	IG1102	7.35	8.40	1234567
MILANO	ROMA	IG1108	8.30	9.35	12345
MILANO	ROMA	IG1104	13.30	14.35	123456
MILANO	ROMA	IG1106	18.30	19.35	123457
ROMA	MILANO	IG1101	9.20	10.25	1234567
ROMA	MILANO	IG1107	15.00	16.05	12345
ROMA	MILANO	IG1103	18.00	19.05	123456
ROMA	MILANO	IG1105	20.35	21.40	123457

Modello   Domanda: Se parto da Milano alle sette e trentacinque a che ora
                          arrivo a Roma?
              Risposta: Alle otto e quaranta.

Now make up some questions of your own based on the timetable.

ESERCIZIO 4.5

Look at the following time chart and work out the corresponding times in the
places mentioned.

GMT	+1	−5	+10
11.00			
	15.00		
		04.00	
			23.00

1 Quando sono le undici a Londra, che ore sono . . .
  a a Roma?
  b a Nuova York?
  c a Sydney?
2 Quando sono le quindici a Roma, che ore sono . . .
  a a Londra?
  b a Nuova York?
  c a Sydney?
3 Quando sono le quattro a Nuova York, che ore sono . . .
  a a Londra?
  b a Roma?
  c a Sydney?
4 Quando sono le ventitrè a Sydney, che ore sono . . .
  a a Londra?
  b a Roma?
  c a Nuova York?

ESERCIZIO 4.6

Simonetta visits a company in England where she meets Benjamin Howell who works in the Sales Department. Listen to the cassette. How would he answer her questions about a typical working day? Remember to use the 24-hour clock throughout.

lunedi	31 Marzo
08.30	START WORK
10.45–11.00	COFFEE BREAK
12.45–13.45	LUNCH
13.45	BACK TO WORK
15.30–15.45	TEA BREAK
17.30	FINISH WORK

SIMONETTA GIORGI: A che ora comincia il lavoro la mattina?
BENJAMIN HOWELL: *At 8.30.*
SIMONETTA GIORGI: E a che ora finisce?
BENJAMIN HOWELL: *At 5.30 in the afternoon. (Use the 24-hour clock.)*
SIMONETTA GIORGI: Non è una giornata troppo lunga. Ci sono pause durante il gio
BENJAMIN HOWELL: *Yes three – at 10.45 for coffee, at 12.45 for lunch and at 15.30 for tea*
SIMONETTA GIORGI: C'è una mensa per il personale nella ditta?
BENJAMIN HOWELL: *Yes, but I prefer to go to a restaurant.*

ESERCIZIO 4.7

Simonetta finds out more about what Benjamin does. Take his part.

SIMONETTA GIORGI: E Lei, che lavoro fa esattamente?
BENJAMIN HOWELL: *I coordinate sales operations, and I am often in contact*
with the sales agents.
SIMONETTA GIORGI: Ho capito. Lei viaggia molto allora?
BENJAMIN HOWELL: *Quite a lot. I visit the branches twice a month.*
SIMONETTA GIORGI: Dove sono le filiali?
BENJAMIN HOWELL: *In Birmingham and Bristol.*
SIMONETTA GIORGI: Sono lontane?
BENJAMIN HOWELL: *Not too far . . . Birmingham is about 65 kilometres and Bristol about 70.*
SIMONETTA GIORGI: E quando Lei è fuori sede, finisce il lavoro alle 17.30?
BENJAMIN HOWELL: *No . . . Often I finish at 10 or 11 o'clock at night.*

ESERCIZIO 4.8

Simonetta finds out what Benjamin likes to do outside work. This time, take the part of Simonetta.

SIMONETTA GIORGI: *What do you do in the evening?*
BENJAMIN HOWELL: Dipende. Vado al bar con gli amici o al cinema.
SIMONETTA GIORGI: *And on Saturday evening?*
BENJAMIN HOWELL: Generalmente vado al ristorante con gli amici e dopo
andiamo in discoteca.
SIMONETTA GIORGI: *Are you interested in music?*
BENJAMIN HOWELL: Sì certo.
SIMONETTA GIORGI: *What type of music?*
BENJAMIN HOWELL: Oh, la musica pop ma anche la musica classica.
Vado anche ai concerti.

Prima di continuare

Before going on to the next chapter, make sure you can

• ask what time things start and finish	*a che ora comincia?*
	a che ora finisce?
• understand the 24-hour clock	*alle ventitrè e quarantacinque*
• know how to say morning, afternoon and evening	*mattina*
	pomeriggio
	sera
• ask pertinent questions	*quanti agenti di vendita ci sono?*
	quanto costa?
	che tipo di computer è?
• talk about what we do	*andiamo in centro*
• ask about what other people do	*a che ora cominciate la mattina?*
• recognise Italian names of cities	*Firenze, Venezia*
• know the days of the week and numbers	*lunedì*
	duecento
• ask permission to do something	*posso telefonare in Inghilterra?*
• say that you cannot do something	*non posso*
• say what you are interested in or not interested in	*mi interessa visitare la ditta*
	non mi interessa molto
• ask if someone wants to do something	*vuoi andare al cinema?*

Al lavoro

AT WORK

> **In this chapter you will learn how to:**
> • use office equipment
> • say that things are not working
> • say that you do not know how to do something
> • ask for help when things go wrong

DIALOGO 1 *Che cosa bisogna fare?*

Michael impara* ad usare il fax. (*imparare)

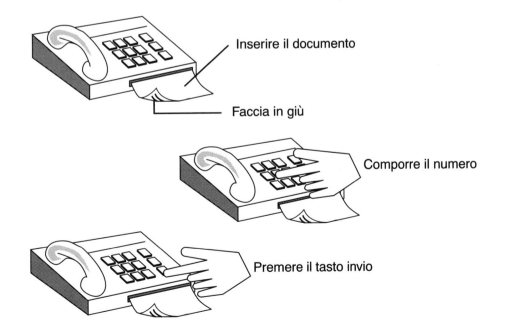

Inserire il documento

Faccia in giù

Comporre il numero

Premere il tasto invio

Michael learns how to use the fax machine.

[cassette] Studiate queste espressioni, ascoltatele e ripetetele nelle pause previste.

adesso	*now*
vediamo* come funziona (vedere)	*let's see how it works*
inserire il documento	*insert the document*
faccia in giù	*face down*
comporre il numero	*dial the number*
premere il tasto invio	*press the start button*
difatti	*in fact*
è molto semplice	*it is very simple*
soltanto	*only*
come si fa?	*what does one do? (lit: how does one do?)*
basta sganciare e selezionare il numero	*all you have to do is lift the receiver and dial (lit: it is sufficient to)*
bisogna comporre il prefisso	*you have to dial the code (lit: it is necessary to)*

[cassette] Adesso chiudete il libro e ascoltate il dialogo.

TOMMASO FIORE: Adesso, vediamo come funziona il fax.
MICHAEL MOOR: Ah sì, è importante.
TOMMASO FIORE: Allora, bisogna inserire il documento faccia in giù; comporre il numero e premere il tasto invio.
MICHAEL MOOR: Non è troppo complicato.
TOMMASO FIORE: Difatti . . . è molto semplice.
MICHAEL MOOR: Va bene . . . e per telefonare . . . come si fa?
TOMMASO FIORE: Per le telefonate interne, basta sganciare e selezionare il numero. Per le telefonate esterne bisogna comporre il prefisso zero e poi il numero.
MICHAEL MOOR: Ho capito.

[cassette] Ascoltate il dialogo di nuovo, questa volta con il libro aperto. Usate il tasto pausa e ripetete ogni frase.

ESERCIZIO 1.1

Choose a role and practise the dialogue with a partner. Move on to another partner and practise the same role. When you feel sure of it, change roles. Repeat the process as many times as you need.

ESERCIZIO 1.2

These are picture instructions for using a telephone. Find the appropriate written instruction underneath for each picture.

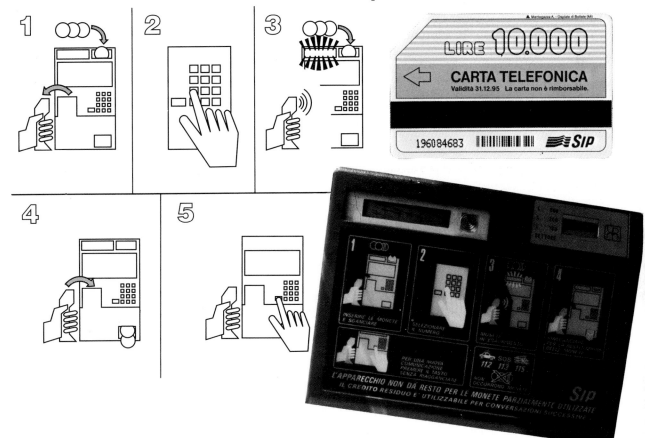

a Selezionare il numero.
b Inserire le monete o la carta e sganciare.
c Riagganciare per la restituzione delle monete (per la restituzione della carta).
d Monete in esaurimento.
e Per una nuova comunicazione premere il tasto senza riagganciare.

DA NOTARE

Remember that before you use your telephone card, you will need to snap off the top left corner as shown above.
It is also useful to know that the SOS numbers stand for the following:

112 polizia	*police*
113 carabinieri	*traffic police*
115 vigili del fuoco	*fire service*

per questi numeri non occorrono monete	*for these numbers no money is required*
l'apparecchio non dà resto per le monete parzialmente utilizzate	*the machine does not give change*
il credito residuo è utilizzabile per conversazioni successivi	*any remaining credit can be used for further calls*

ESERCIZIO 1.3

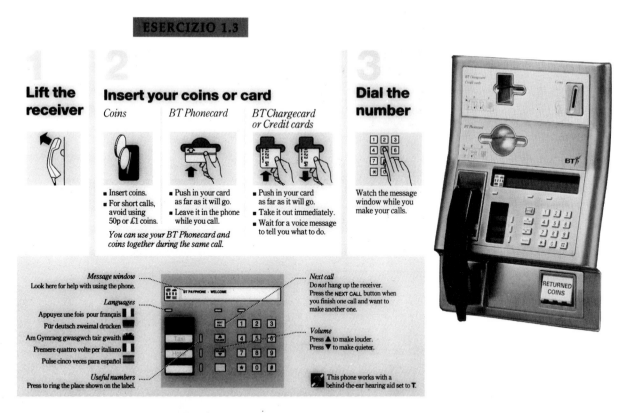

1 Lift the receiver

2 Insert your coins or card

Coins
- Insert coins.
- For short calls, avoid using 50p or £1 coins.

BT Phonecard
- Push in your card as far as it will go.
- Leave it in the phone while you call.

You can use your BT Phonecard and coins together during the same call.

BT Chargecard or Credit cards
- Push in your card as far as it will go.
- Take it out immediately.
- Wait for a voice message to tell you what to do.

3 Dial the number
Watch the message window while you make your calls.

Message window
Look here for help with using the phone.

Languages
Appuyez une fois pour français
Für deutsch zweimal drücken
Am Gymraeg gwasgwch tair gwaith
Premere quattro volte per italiano
Pulse cinco veces para español

Useful numbers
Press to ring the place shown on the label.

Next call
Do *not* hang up the receiver.
Press the NEXT CALL button when you finish one call and want to make another one.

Volume
Press ▲ to make louder.
Press ▼ to make quieter.

This phone works with a behind-the-ear hearing aid set to **T**.

This is a British public telephone. Look at the Italian instructions in *Esercizio 1.2.* Which phrase or part of a phrase most nearly corresponds to the English instructions?

1 Lift handset
2 Insert card
3 Dial number
4 Replace handset
5 Retrieve card

ESERCIZIO 1.4

Identify the following activities by choosing the six most suitable captions from the list of suggestions below.

a

b

1 fare una telefonata
2 usare il computer
3 parlare italiano
4 arrivare in ufficio alle otto
5 fare una fotocopia
6 visitare un museo
7 mandare una lettera

ESERCIZIO 1.5

Look at the list of suggestions in *Esercizio 1.4* and decide how you would
describe each one of them from the following choice of phrases.

è facile   è difficile   è complicato   è semplice   è interessante   è non complicato

Modello   Fare una telefonata è semplice.

DA NOTARE   To say what has to be done, use *bisogna*.

bisogna mandare un fax   (*lit: it is necessary to send a fax*)

To say, 'all you have to do is . . .', use *basta*.

basta telefonare   (*lit: it is sufficient to phone*)

ESERCIZIO 1.6

Look at the list of suggestions in *Esercizio 1.4* and choose a phrase to complete the following sentences.

Modello   Stimolo: Per sapere se Tommaso Fiore è disponibile, bisogna . . .
                Risposta: Bisogna fare una telefonata.

1 Per sapere se Matteo Cerulli è disponibile, bisogna . . .
2 Per vedere delle belle statue, bisogna . . .
3 Quando si va in Italia, bisogna . . .
4 Per trovare l'indirizzo di questo cliente, bisogna . . .
5 Se mandate questa lettera a Tommaso e a Simonetta, bisogna . . . per me.

ESERCIZIO 1.7

Listen to the prompts on cassette. If you find yourself in the following difficulties, what should you do? You will find some suggestions below.

Modello   Stimolo: Se non capisce?   *If you don't understand?*
                Risposta: Basta chiedere.   *All you have to do is ask.*

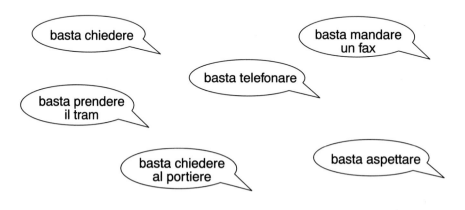

DIALOGO 2 *Mi può aiutare?*

La fotocopiatrice non funziona.

The photocopier is not working.

 Studiate queste espressioni, ascoltatele e ripetetele nelle pause previste.

devo fare una telefonata	*I have to make a phone call*
mi può?	*can you do something for me?*
cosa significa?* (significare)	*what does it mean?*
aspetti* un momento (aspettare)	*wait a moment*
a presto	*see you soon (or hear from you soon)*
non c'è più carta	*there's no more paper*
qui sotto	*under here*
per l'archivio	*for the file*

 Adesso chiudete il libro e ascoltate il dialogo.

TOMMASO FIORE: Devo fare una telefonata. Mi può fotocopiare questo documento, per favore?

MICHAEL MOOR: Certo. . . . *Blast!* . . . Signor Fiore, scusi, ma non funziona. Cosa significa la luce rossa?

TOMMASO FIORE: Aspetti un momento. . . . Sì, ciao Adriano, a presto. Mmm, non c'è più carta. C'è carta qui sotto.

MICHAEL MOOR: Grazie. Ora va bene. Quante copie?

TOMMASO FIORE: Due: una per l'archivio e una per l'agente.

 Ascoltate il dialogo di nuovo, questa volta con il libro aperto. Usate il tasto pausa e ripetete ogni frase.

ESERCIZIO 2.1

Choose a role and practise the dialogue with a partner. Move on to another partner and practise the same role. When you feel sure of it, change roles. Repeat the process as many times as you need.

DA NOTARE

What should you do when things do not go well? Here are some useful expressions.

mi dispiace ma *I'm sorry but . . .*

non so	*I don't know*	come funziona questo	*how this works*
		come fare questo	*how to do this*
non capisco	*I don't understand*	perché non funziona	*why it is not working*
		quando bisogna comporre il numero	*when you have to dial*
		dove devo inserire la carta	*where I have to insert the paper*

Non so and *non capisco* are often interchangeable.

ESERCIZIO 2.2

You are having a bad day. Look at the expressions in *Da notare* above. Choose an appropriate one, or adapt one, to express how you might feel in the following circumstances.

GRAMMATICA

Verb categories

So far we have learnt verbs as we have come across them. It would now be useful to recognise that there are four main categories of verbs in Italian, those ending in *are*, those in *ere*, and two ending in *ire*. Most verbs follow a predictable pattern according to their ending, and endings are particularly important in Italian because they tell you who or what is doing the action of the verb.

	are	**ere**	**ire (a)**	**ire (b)**
	arriv**are**	prend**ere**	part**ire**	cap**ire**
	to arrive	*to take*	*to leave*	*to understand*
I	arriv**o**	prend**o**	part**o**	cap**isco**
you (inf)	arriv**i**	prend**i**	part**i**	cap**isci**
you (for)	arriv**a**	prend**e**	part**e**	cap**isce**
he/she/it	arriv**a**	prend**e**	part**e**	cap**isce**
we	arriv**iamo**	prend**iamo**	part**iamo**	cap**iamo**
you (pl)	arriv**ate**	prend**ete**	part**ite**	cap**ite**
they	arriv**ano**	prend**ono**	part**ono**	cap**iscono**

devo is irregular and is part of the verb *dovere* 'to have to':

devo	*I have to*
devi	*You (inf) have to*
Lei deve	*you (for) have to*
deve	*he, she has to*
dobbiamo	*we have to*
dovete	*you (pl) have to*
devono	*they have to*

ESERCIZIO 2.3

This is Tommaso Fiore's timetable for today.

lunedì	31 Marzo
mattina	9.00 partire per Brescia 11.30 appuntamento con Alessi
pomeriggio	14.00 tornare a Bologna 15.00 vedere Matteo NB mandare il fax a Londra per confermare l'ordine della Habitat
sera	21.00 incontrare Simonetta davanti al cinema

Tommaso's sister phones to check on his arrangements for today. Listen to the cassette and answer the questions as if you were Tommaso.

ESERCIZIO 2.4

Notice how Tommaso asks Michael to do something for him, *Mi può fare una fotocopia, per favore?* You find yourself in difficulties so ask a colleague for help in the following situations.

Modello   Stimolo: Devo fare una telefonata ma non parlo bene l'italiano.
Risposta: Mi può fare una telefonata per piacere?

1 Devo fare una telefonata ma non parlo bene l'italiano.
2 Devo mandare questo fax, ma non so il numero.
3 Devo fare una fotocopia ma non so usare la fotocopiatrice.
4 Devo accendere il computer, ma non so come.
5 Devo scrivere una lettera ma non so scrivere in italiano.

ESERCIZIO 2.5

Making educated guesses is a skill of the successful language learner. Nothing is working in the office today. The complaints are listed in the left-hand column. On the right is a series of reasons or solutions. Can you match the two columns? In case of difficulty, consult the vocabulary at the back of the book.

1 Il fax non parte.
2 La fotocopiatrice non funziona.
3 Il telefono non risponde.
4 Il computer non funziona.

a Bisogna comporre il prefisso.
b Non c'è carta.
c Bisogna premere il tasto invio.
d Non è acceso.

ESERCIZIO 2.6

DEAR VISITOR, WELCOME TO ITALY!!!

Aeroporti di Roma is glad to provide you with some useful information on how to place international telephone calls as well as telephone calls within Italy.

INTERNATIONAL DIRECT DIALING

There are different ways you can call:

PAY NOW

To call direct from Italy the dialing sequence is:

00	COUNTRY CODE	AREA CODE	LOCAL NUMBER

Example:

00	1 U.S.A.	617 BOSTON	xxxxxxx

Countries that can be direct dialed are:

● ALGERIA	213	CAMEROON	237
ANGOLA	244	CANADA	1
ARGENTINA	54	CHILE	56
AUSTRALIA	61	CHINA	86
● AUSTRIA	43	COLOMBIA	57
BAHAMAS	851	COSTA RICA	506
BAHRAIN	973	CUBA	53
BANGLADESH	880	● CYPRUS	357
BELGIUM	32	● CZECHOSLOVAKIA	42
BERMUDA	851	● DENMARK	45
BOLIVIA	591	DJIBOUTI	253
BRAZIL	55	DOMINICAN REP.	851

ECUADOR	593	NORWAY	47
EGYPT	20	OMAN	968
ETHIOPIA	251	PAKISTAN	92
● FAROER IS.	298	PANAMA	507
FINLAND	358	PARAGUAY	595
● FRANCE	33	PERU	51
GABON	241	PHILIPPINES	63
● GERMANY (EAST)	37	● POLAND	48
● GERMANY (WEST)	49	● PORTUGAL	351
● GREECE	30	PUERTO RICO	851
GUATEMALA	502	QATAR	974
HAWAII	1	RUMANIA	40
HONDURAS	504	SAUDI ARABIA	966
HONG KONG	852	SENEGAL	221
● HUNGARY	36	SEYCHELLES IS.	248
● ICELAND	354	SINGAPORE	65
INDIA	91	SOMALIA	252
INDONESIA	62	SOUTH AFRICA	27
IRAN	98	SOUTH KOREA	82
IRAQ	964	SPAIN	34
● IRELAND	353	SRI LANKA	94
ISRAEL	972	● SWEDEN	46
IVORY COAST	225	● SWITZERLAND	41
JAPAN	81	SYRIA	963
JORDAN	962	TAIWAN	886
KENYA	254	TANZANIA	255
KUWAIT	965	THAILAND	66
● LIBYA	218	TUNISIA	216
● LIECHTENSTEIN	41	● TURKEY	90
● LUXEMBURG	352	UN. ARAB EMIRATES	971
MADAGASCAR	261	● UNITED KINGDOM	44
MALAYSIA	60	URUGUAY	598
● MALTA	356	U.S.A.	1
MAURITIUS IS.	230	VENEZUELA	58
● MEXICO	52	VIRGIN ISLANDS	851
● MONACO	33	YEMEN ARAB REP.	967
● MOROCCO	212	● YUGOSLAVIA	38
● NETHERLANDS	31	ZAMBIA	260
NEW ZEALAND	64	ZIMBABWE	263
NIGERIA	234		

REDUCED RATE: 11 PM TO 8 AM - SUNDAY ALL-DAY
● 10 PM TO 8 AM - SUNDAY ALL DAY

PUBLIC PAYPHONES

Standard payphones accept 100, 200 and 500 lire coins and or special telephone tokens. We recommend a minimum of 3,000 lire when calling outside Italy.

Phonecard payphones accept a pre-paid card available in units of 5,000 or 10,000 lire: you may find them at airports, railway stations, newspaper stands, tobacconists, post offices, etc.

PHONING WITHIN ITALY

For calls within Italy, you'll find that all telephone numbers have an area code starting with 0, and then a local number.

If calling within the area, you omit the area code.

For example, the Rome code is 06:
you dial it when calling from another city
you don't when calling inside the Rome area

What is the code? *Qual'è il prefisso?* From the information available, can you answer the questions below?

1 Qual'è il prefisso internazionale?
2 Qual'è il prefisso per la Gran Bretagna?
3 Qual'è il prefisso per gli Stati Uniti di America?
4 Per fare una telefonata internazionale, quanto denaro bisogna avere?
5 Quanto costano le carte telefoniche?

DA NOTARE

Whereas *posso* means, 'I am (physically) able to do something', *so* means, 'I know how to do something'.

posso contattare Giorgio stasera	*I can contact Giorgio this evening*
so usare il computer	*I can use the computer (I know how to use the computer)*

ESERCIZIO 2.7

Which would you use in the following sentences: *posso* or *so*?

1 .... parlare italiano.
2 .... usare il fax.
3 .... venire a cena venerdì.
4 .... andare in centro in autobus.
5 .... mandare questa lettera in Inghilterra.
6 .... scrivere l'indirizzo.

GRAMMATICA   *sapere* – 'to know' **or** 'to know how to'

This is another verb that does not follow a set pattern and has to be learnt.

so	*I*
sai	*you (inf)*
sa	*you (for)*
sa	*he, she or it*
sappiamo	*we*
sapete	*you (pl)*
sanno	*they*

DIALOGO 3 *Com'è organizzato?*

Com'è organizzato lo schedario?

How is the filing cabinet organised?

 Studiate queste espressioni, ascoltatele e ripetetele nelle pause previste.

lo schedario	*the filing cabinet*
la corrispondenza	*the correspondence*
com'è organizzato?	*how is it organised?*
è diviso	*it is divided*
conserviamo* (conservare)	*we keep*
ad esempio	*for example*
in questo cassetto	*in this drawer*
in ordine alfabetico	*in alphabetical order*
archiviare	*to file*

 Adesso chiudete il libro e ascoltate il dialogo.

TOMMASO FIORE: Questo è lo schedario. Qui c'è la corrispondenza con i clienti in Italia.

MICHAEL MOOR: Com'è organizzato lo schedario?

TOMMASO FIORE: È diviso per filiali ed agenti.

MICHAEL MOOR: Ad esempio, cosa c'è in questo cassetto?

TOMMASO FIORE: Qui conserviamo la corrispondenza di tutti i clienti della filiale di Brescia.

MICHAEL MOOR: Sono in ordine alfabetico, vero?

TOMMASO FIORE: Sì, esatto. Infatti sotto la lettera 'c', possiamo archiviare questo documento del signor Colombini.

 Ascoltate il dialogo di nuovo, questa volta con il libro aperto. Usate il tasto pausa e ripetete ogni frase.

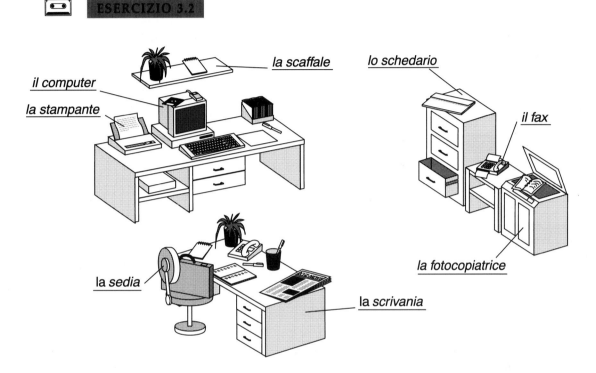

ESERCIZIO 3.1

Choose a role and practise the dialogue with a partner. Move on to another partner and practise the same role. When you feel sure of it, change roles. Repeat the process as many times as you need.

ESERCIZIO 3.2

la scaffale   lo schedario

il computer

la stampante

il fax

la fotocopiatrice

la sedia

la scrivania

Look at the picture above. On each of the larger pieces of equipment, you will see smaller items, e.g. a pen, briefcase etc. Now listen to the cassette very carefully as many times as you wish, and see if you can identify what the following pieces of smaller equipment are.

1 foglio	4 dossier	7 ventiquattrore	10 dischetto
2 matita	5 libro	8 mouse	11 agenda
3 penna	6 carta	9 bloc-notes	12 giornale

ESERCIZIO 3.3

Listen to the cassette once more and fill in the gaps below.

1 Sulla fotocopiatrice, c'è un ....
2 Sul fax c'è un ....
3 Sullo schedario c'è un ....
4 Sulla scrivania c'è un'........., una ...., una .... e un ....
5 Sulla sedia, c'è una ....
6 Sul computer, c'è un .... e una ....
7 Sullo scaffale, c'è un ....
8 Sulla stampante, c'è ....

📼 **ESERCIZIO 3.4**

L'alfabeto in italiano. Listen to the alphabet on cassette and repeat in the pauses provided.

📼 **ESERCIZIO 3.5**

Read the following names. How would you spell them out to someone in Italian? For double letters, e.g. *ll* say, *doppia elle*.

1 Cerulli	**2** Fiore	**3** Giorgi
4 Olivetti	**5** Moor	**6** Colombini

Listen to the cassette to check that you have done it correctly.

DA NOTARE   Usually when people require you to spell your name in Italy, they ask:

come si scrive?   *how do you spell it?*

DA NOTARE   *Where exactly is it?*

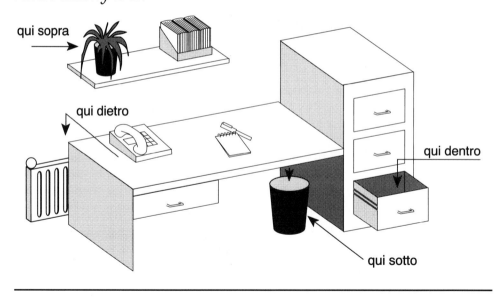

📼 **ESERCIZIO 3.6**

Listen to the prompts on cassette and ask the necessary questions. Decide whether the objects you are looking for are on, under, inside or behind the objects mentioned in the replies. In the column on the right, note the objects mentioned in the replies.

Modello   Stimolo: *Ask where the paper is.*
              Domanda: Dov'è la carta?
              Riposta: Qui sotto – sotto la stampante.

	sopra	sotto	dentro	dietro	oggetto
1		✓			la stampante
2					
3					
4					
5					
6					

ESERCIZIO 3.7

C'è or *ci sono*? *C'è* means, 'there is' and *ci sono* means, 'there are'. Which would you use in the following circumstances?

1 .... venti dossier in questo cassetto.
2 .... anche una lista degli agenti in Lombardia.
3 .... venti regioni in Italia.
4 Non .... tempo per fare questo.
5 Non .... biglietti per il teatro stasera.
6 .... un treno per Milano alle 17.30.

ESERCIZIO 3.8

The two pictures below are almost identical. Can you spot the differences? Write them out in Italian.

1   **2**

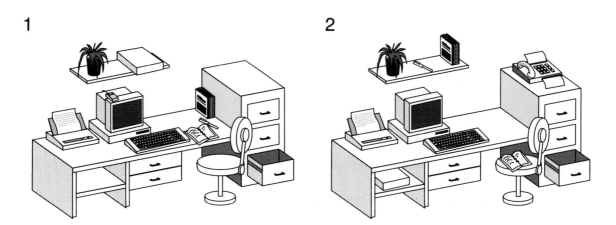

	nel primo disegno	**nel secondo disegno**
1		
2		
3		
4		
5		

DIALOGO 4   *C'è un problema*

PRESENTAZIONE

Mi chiamo Francesco Sabatini. Abito a
Bari ma sono di Taranto. Ho
trentacinque anni. Sono sposato e ho
due bambini; un figlio di quattro anni
e una figlia di due anni.

Un agente di vendita arriva da Bari per vedere Tommaso Fiore.

A sales representative arrives from Bari to see Tommaso Fiore.

 Studiate queste espressioni, ascoltatele e ripetetele nelle pause previste.

avanti	*come in (or come forward)*
come stai?	*how are you?*
non c'è male	*not bad*
l'affare	*business deal*
mi pare	*it seems to me*
lo credo anch'io	*I think so too*
una richiesta	*a request*
si tratta	*it concerns*
che cosa ne pensa	*what he thinks about it*
venga!	*come! (when addressing someone formally)*

Adesso chiudete il libro e ascoltate il dialogo.

FRANCESCO SABATINI:	Permesso? Posso?
TOMMASO FIORE:	Ah, Francesco, avanti, avanti, come stai?
FRANCESCO SABATINI:	Io bene, grazie e tu?
TOMMASO FIORE	Insomma, non c'è male. Sei qui per l'affare del tuo cliente? Mi pare interessante . . .
FRANCESCO SABATINI:	Lo credo anch'io . . . Abbiamo una richiesta per quaranta scrivanie con sedie.
TOMMASO FIORE:	Benissimo. Si tratta del modello Manhattan, vero?
FRANCESCO SABATINI:	Sì, ma c'è un problema. Il cliente preferisce quattro cassetti invece di tre.
TOMMASO FIORE:	Mmm. Andiamo a vedere che cosa ne pensa l'ingegner Bordone. Michael, venga anche Lei!

Ascoltate il dialogo di nuovo, questa volta con il libro aperto. Usate il tasto pausa e ripetete ogni frase.

ESERCIZIO 4.1

Choose a role and practise the dialogue with a partner. Move on to another partner and practise the same role. When you feel sure of it, change roles. Repeat the process as many times as you need.

DA NOTARE   When meeting people you know, it is usual to ask how they are. In Italian there are two ways of doing this.

To a friend, a peer, member of the family or someone younger
Come stai?

To someone you would address more formally
Come sta?

The answer depends on how you feel.

molto bene, grazie	bene	abbastanza bene	non c'è male	sto proprio male

Insomma is a very useful word because it can mean almost any of the above depending on the tone of voice used.

ESERCIZIO 4.2

Listen to the short conversations on cassette. In each one, *insomma* is used to convey a different meaning. Can you decide what it means each time before you are told on cassette?

ESERCIZIO 4.3

Listen to the conversations on cassette and decide how the people are feeling on a scale of 4 to 0: 4 – very well, 3 – well, 2 – quite well, 1 – not too bad, 0 – poorly.

	4	3	2	1	0
Anna					
Giovanni					
Caterina					
Daniele					
Claudio					
Camilla					

ESERCIZIO 4.4

Abitare means, 'to live'; *dove abita?* (formal) or *dove abiti?* (informal) mean, 'where do you live?' We have already seen that *di dov'è* or *di dove sei?* mean, 'where are you from originally?'

Now listen to the cassette and decide where these people are living now and where they came from originally.

	Born in	Now living at
Anna		
Giovanni		
Caterina		
Daniele		
Claudio		
Camilla		

ESERCIZIO 4.5

Which of the following would you use in the phrases below: *posso, puoi, può,* or *possiamo*?

1 Signor Fiore, mi .... passare l'agenda, per favore?
2 Michael ed io .... andare in centro dopo pranzo.
3 Io .... telefonare in Inghilterra?
4 Simonetta, ... venire al cinema con me stasera?
5 Mi dispiace, ma non .... Devo lavorare fino a tardi.

ESERCIZIO 4.6

You need to be absolutely sure how things work. Check with Tommaso.

1 Che cosa devo fare per ....
in Inghilterra?

4 .... trovo la carta per la fotocopiatrice?

2 Com'è .... questo schedario?

5 .... faccio per accendere la stampante?

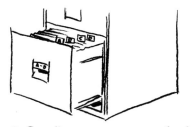 

3 Come .... il fax?

6 Perché non .... il computer?

ESERCIZIO 4.7

Listen to the prompts on cassette. Ask Tommaso about the problems you are facing and listen to his replies.

Modello Stimolo: *Ask why the computer isn't working.*
             Domanda: Perché non funziona il computer?
             Risposta: Non è acceso. Il tasto è qui a destra.

In the grid below, list each problem with its cause or solution.

	Problem	Cause or solution
1		
2		
3		
4		
5		

ESERCIZIO 4.8

a 1 What has the *telefono azzurro* been set up to protect?
2 What are you sending away for?
3 Where will you send the slip?

Desidero ricevere il depliant informativo gratuito sulla vostra attività e sulle possibilità di collaborazione.

NOME _____ COGNOME _____
VIA _____ CAP _____
CITTÀ _____ PROV. _____ TEL. _____
Inviare a Telefono Azzurro, Via dell'Angelo
Custode, 1\3-40141 Bologna

IL TELEFONO AZZURRO 051·222525

Linea diretta in difesa dell'infanzia e dell'adolescenza

b 1 What three steps do you need to follow when using this card?

SCOPRITE SUBITO I VANTAGGI DELLA CARTA DI CREDITO TELEFONICA.

Oggi è possibile telefonare in teleselezione, in Italia e all'estero, da qualsiasi telefono pubblico dotato di apposito lettore, senza limiti di spesa e di tempo.

FACILE DA USARE.

Inserita la carta nel lettore, è sufficiente comporre il Vostro codice personale e, di seguito, il numero desiderato.

c 1 What can you save for tomorrow while you fly today?
2 For every business trip to Washington what might you therefore gain?

Mileage Plus. Mentre volate oggi, accumulate già miglia per domani.

Con Mileage Plus, il frequent flyer program United, accumulate velocemente miglia su miglia, da usare a vostro piacere. Così, ad esempio, in ogni viaggio di lavoro a Washington c'è già un po' di vacanza alle Hawaii.

AIR BUSINESS CENTRE

d 1 What can you organise in the airport?
2 What will you be able to utilise better?
3 How will you be able to be contacted?
4 Is there a translation service?
5 Would you be able to book a hotel from there?

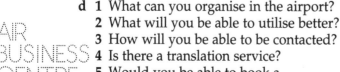

Vi permette di:

• organizzare riunioni e incontri direttamente in aeroporto

• utilizzare al meglio i tempi d'attesa

• essere reperibili in aeroporto, telefonicamente o via fax

• essere assistiti da esperte segretarie per: contatti telefonici, lavori di videoscrittura, fax, fotocopie, traduzioni, hostess

• prenotazioni e informazioni: alberghi, ristoranti, autonoleggi, residence, uffici residence, spedizioni

ESERCIZIO 4.9

Student A will take the part of Francesco Sabatini and Student B that of Simonetta Giorgi. Imagine that you meet for the first time at an office party. What will you say to each other? Your conversation should include some of the following suggestions:

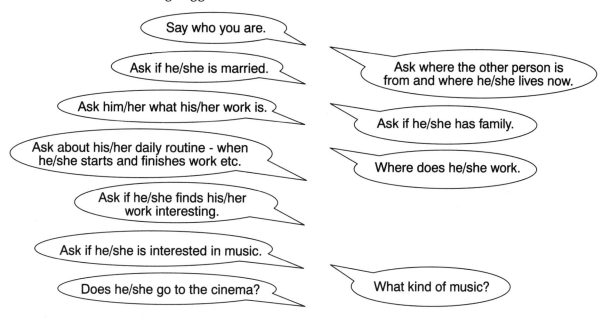

Say who you are.

Ask if he/she is married.

Ask where the other person is from and where he/she lives now.

Ask him/her what his/her work is.

Ask if he/she has family.

Ask about his/her daily routine - when he/she starts and finishes work etc.

Where does he/she work.

Ask if he/she finds his/her work interesting.

Ask if he/she is interested in music.

Does he/she go to the cinema?

What kind of music?

ESERCIZIO 4.10

This set of exercises may be used in a variety of ways, such as for paired work or as a revision exercise on cassette.

Michael Moor is now working for a firm in Britain and is asked to make a phone call to Italsistemi in Italy to confirm an order. Take the part of Michael Moor.

PORTIERE:	Pronto ... Chi parla?
LEI:	*I am Michael Moor from London. Can I speak to Tommaso Fiore?*
PORTIERE:	Certo ... resti in linea, per favore ...
TOMMASO FIORE:	Pronto ... Tommaso Fiore ...
LEI:	*Hello, Tommaso, how are you? I am Michael Moor.*
TOMMASO FIORE:	Buongiorno, Michael. Come sta? Cosa posso fare per Lei?
LEI:	*It's about the order for desks ...*
TOMMASO FIORE:	Ah sì il modello Manhattan, vero?
LEI:	*Yes, we want to confirm the order for 20 desks. Is that OK?*
TOMMASO FIORE:	Sì, va bene ma bisogna anche mandare un fax.
LEI:	*Certainly, I'll do it straight away.*
TOMMASO FIORE:	Ha il numero?
LEI:	*Yes, 00 39 51 39 83 52 76.*
TOMMASO FIORE:	Bene. Allora a presto, Michael. Tante belle cose ... Ciao!
LEI:	*Bye, Tommaso.*

ESERCIZIO 4.11

Tommaso's secretary brings him the fax from Michael. You take the part of the secretary, Marta Manzini. You are relatively new here.

MARTA MANZINI: *Mr Fiore, there is a fax for you from London.*

TOMMASO FIORE: Ah sì, da Michael. È un ordine per venti scrivanie. Mi può fare due fotocopie, per favore?

MARTA MANZINI: *Of course. Hm, there's no more paper. Where is the paper for the photocopier?*

TOMMASO FIORE: È sullo scaffale a destra.

MARTA MANZINI: *Thank you. Here are the two copies. Do I have to file this one?*

TOMMASO FIORE: Sì per piacere. E poi facciamo una richiesta di disponibilità merce all'ufficio magazzino.

MARTA MANZINI: *Certainly, straight away.*

ESERCIZIO 4.12

The availability of the merchandise is confirmed and Tommaso asks Marta to phone England. You take Marta's part.

TOMMASO FIORE: Signorina Manzini, Lei sa parlare inglese, vero?

MARTA MANZINI: *Well, yes I can speak, but not very well.*

TOMMASO FIORE: Può chiamare Michael, per piacere?

MARTA MANZINI: *OK. What is the number?*

TOMMASO FIORE: È a Londra – 171 325 679.

MARTA MANZINI: *And what is the code for England?*

TOMMASO FIORE: È zero, zero, quarantaquattro.

MARTA MANZINI: *It is not working. I don't understand when you have to dial.*

TOMMASO FIORE: Dopo zero, zero quarantaquattro, bisogna aspettare un attimo.

MARTA MANZINI: *Now it's working.*

Prima di continuare

Before going on to Chapter 5, make sure that you can:

• understand instructions	*sganciare*
	selezionare/comporre il numero
• ask questions about how things work	*come funziona?*
	com'è organizzato
• say what you have to do	*devo fare una telefonata*
• ask someone to do something for you	*mi può fotocopiare questo?*
• say that something is not working	*non funziona il computer*
• understand why it is not working	*non è acceso*
• find out exactly where things are	*su, sotto, dietro, dentro*

Lavorare da solo

In this chapter you will learn how to:
- use the company's database
- phone for assistance
- sort out a problem
- help a visitor

DIALOGO 1 *Sa usare la banca dati?*

Tommaso chiede* a Michael di usare la banca dati. (*chiedere)

Tommaso asks Michael to use the database.

Studiate queste espressioni, ascoltatele e ripetetele nelle pause previste.

sa* usare . . . ? (sapere)	*can you use . . . ?*
credo di sì	*I think so*
mi può* trovare (potere)	*can you find me . . . ?*
ora vado* (andare)	*I am going now*

 Adesso chiudete il libro e ascoltate il dialogo.

> TOMMASO FIORE: Michael, sa usare la banca dati?
> MICHAEL MOOR: Credo di sì.
> TOMMASO FIORE: Mi può trovare l'indirizzo di questi clienti di Bari?
> MICHAEL MOOR: Va bene. Che password usate qui?
> TOMMASO FIORE: 'Benvenuti alla Italsistemi'. Per terminare bisogna premere il tasto 'Ritorno' o 'Uscita'.
> MICHAEL MOOR: Grazie. La stampante è accesa?
> TOMMASO FIORE: Sì. Ora vado dal dottor Cerulli. Buon lavoro, Michael!

 Ascoltate il dialogo di nuovo, questa volta con il libro aperto. Usate il tasto pausa e ripetete ogni frase.

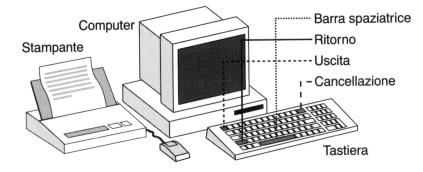

ESERCIZIO 1.1

Choose a role and practise the dialogue with a partner. Move on to another partner and practise the same role. When you feel sure of it, change roles. Repeat the process as many times as you need.

 ### ESERCIZIO 1.2

Listen to the people on the cassette. Each of them makes either a statement or asks a question. Remember that there is no difference in the way the sentence looks when it is written down, but in speech it is important to make the difference clear through intonation. Try and establish whether what you hear is a statement or a question and tick the appropriate row.

	1	2	3	4	5	6
Statement						
Question						

ESERCIZIO 1.3

Listen to each statement and question again and practise the intonation either on your own or with a partner, first as a statement, then as a question.

DA NOTARE You may remember that when asking a colleague or an acquaintance or a passerby to do something for you, the expression *mi può* + infinitive verb is used.

> **mi può spegnere** la stampante?
> **mi può inserire** i nuovi ordini nella banca dati?
> **mi può indicare** dov'è il tasto 'Ritorno'?

Michael and Simonetta, who have a more informal working relationship, would use *mi puoi* (+ infinitive verb) when addressing each other.

Michael, **mi puoi passare** il dischetto, per favore?

ESERCIZIO 1.4

CONTATTARE AGENTI NAPOLI

MANDARE FAX A MONACO

CONFERMARE FIERA A NOVEMBRE

TELEFONARE ING. BORDONE

Matteo Cerulli leaves a message on the answerphone for Simonetta asking her to do a few things for him during his absence. Simonetta has jotted this down in a hurry. Do you think she has got everything right? Listen to Matteo and check Simonetta's notes below:

Now compare your notes with a

ESERCIZIO 1.5

Now work with a partner and practise asking each other (nicely!) to do a few things.

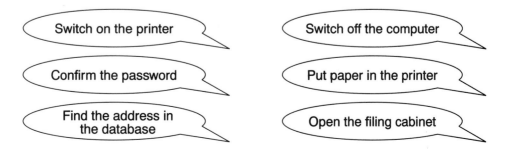

Switch on the printer

Switch off the computer

Confirm the password

Put paper in the printer

Find the address in the database

Open the filing cabinet

ESERCIZIO 1.6

Look at this electronic notebook and answer the questions:

1 What is planned for 3 p.m.?
2 What needs to be done at 4.30 p.m.?
3 Why is Roberto very unlikely to take part in any office activity today?

DIALOGO 2   *Aiuto!*

Michael è confuso e telefona a Simonetta.

Michael is confused and calls Simonetta on the phone.

Studiate queste espressioni, ascoltatele e ripetetele nelle pause previste.

interno 320	*extension 320*
al telefono	*on the phone*
dimmi* (dire)	*tell me (go ahead)*
non trovo* (trovare)	*I cannot find*
la scrittura	*handwriting*
sei sicuro?	*are you sure?*
non cancellare	*don't delete*

Adesso chiudete il libro e ascoltate il dialogo.

MICHAEL MOOR:	Pronto, interno 320? Sono Michael Moor. C'è Simonetta?
VOICE:	Simonetta! C'è Michael al telefono.
SIMONETTA GIORGI:	Ciao, Michael, dimmi . . .
MICHAEL MOOR:	Pronto, Simonetta, sono Michael. C'è un problema con la banca dati e Tommaso non c'è . . . Devo trovare i dati di un cliente, Ollimondi, ma non trovo il nome.
SIMONETTA GIORGI:	Ollimondi . . . sei sicuro?
MICHAEL MOOR	Forse non capisco la scrittura di Tommaso . . .
SIMONETTA GIORGI:	Va bene, arrivo subito. Non cancellare i dati!

```
MENU PRINCIPALE
"ITALSISTEMI VENDITE"

Opzioni    ITV1 Sede Centrale

           ITV2 Filiali

           ITV3 Clienti
```

Ascoltate il dialogo di nuovo, questa volta con il libro aperto. Usate il tasto pausa e ripetete ogni frase.

ESERCIZIO 2.1

Choose a role and practise the dialogue with a partner. Move on to another partner and practise the same role. When you feel sure of it, change roles. Repeat the process as many times as you need.

ESERCIZIO 2.2

Listen again to the dialogue without looking at the text and check whether the statements below are true or false.

Vero   Falso

1 Simonetta è in ufficio con Michael.
2 Tommaso ha un problema con la banca dati.
3 Michael non trova i dati di un cliente.
4 Michael consulta Simonetta.
5 Simonetta offre subito di aiutare Michael.

Today is one of those days; everybody in the office is running around looking stressed. What's the problem? Listen to the cassette and find out.

1 the secretary
2 the sales director
3 the technician
4 the receptionist
5 the agent

ESERCIZIO 2.4

Many Italian companies now advertise a *Numero Verde*. Name three advantages for the caller.

CHIEDERE NON COSTA NULLA

SENZA PREFISSO, SENZA PAGARE PUOI CHIAMARE DA QUALUNQUE APPARECCHIO TELEFONICO TUTTE LE AZIENDE CHE HANNO IL NUMERO VERDE.

CHIAMATA GRATUITA'
NUMEROVERDE
1678 - 00001

SIP

GRAMMATICA

The imperative

In *Dialogo* 2 Simonetta tells Michael not to cancel the data (*non cancellare i dati!*).

When addressing someone informally the negative form of the imperative is obtained by using *non* followed by the infinitive.

non toccare la presa
non usare la fotocopiatrice
non cancellare nulla

ESERCIZIO 2.5

Listen to the cassette. Tommaso Fiore has received a telephone call from a new agent who is having difficulties with a client. Listen and try to work out what advice he gives the agent by filling in the gaps.

1 Non .... le difficoltà.
2 È meglio .... di persona.
3 Non .... con la sua segretaria.
4 Non .... le sue condizioni.
5 Non .... di portare la pubblicità.

ESERCIZIO 2.6

Work with a partner. Each of you has come across a slight problem. Ask your partner for assistance but be prepared also to give your partner some advice. Use one item from each column as appropriate to make up the sentences.

Modello Domanda: C'è un problema: non trovo l'indirizzo del cliente. Cosa faccio?
          Risposta: È semplice: bisogna cercare nella banca dati.

non c'è	l'accento		stampante
non trovo	la stampante	di	Simonetta
non capisco	la barra	per la	Bologna
non vedo	la scrittura	sulla	scrivania
non ho	l'agenda	della	filiale
non funziona	carta		spaziatrice
			tastiera

è semplice	bisogna	chiedere a Simonetta
	basta	mettere altra carta
		ascoltare con attenzione
		premere più forte
		chiedere ai colleghi
		telefonare alla filiale

ESERCIZIO 2.7

Listen to the prompts on cassette. A colleague is asking for your opinion or help. What advice would you give?

Modello Stimolo: C'è una luce rossa nella fotocopiatrice. Cosa faccio?
          Risposta: Non fotocopiare per cinque minuti.

ESERCIZIO 2.8

When working and socialising in Italy you may find that many Italians express a personal interest in a foreign visitor. Fairly direct questions are often asked, such as the ones below. Start practising your answers now with a partner!

Modello

1 Va al bar con Simonetta?
2 Ha un'agenda elettronica?
3 Ha una ragazza/un ragazzo in Inghiterra?
4 Conosce il fidanzato di Simonetta?
5 È tifoso di calcio?
6 Le interessa la politica italiana?
7 Sa guidare una moto?
8 Cosa fa di solito la domenica?

ESERCIZIO 2.9

It is now your turn to express a polite interest in your colleagues by asking questions about them. Listen to the prompts on cassette to ask the questions.

Modello Stimolo: Cosa fa la sera, signor Bini?
Risposta: Di solito guardo la televisione.

ESERCIZIO 2.10

Look at these two adverts for portable phones. What are their best-selling features?

Caratteristiche	Swatch cellular	Swatch twintam
Tre colori		
Batteria ecologica		
Segreteria telefonica		
Quattro colori		
Memoria di venti numeri		
Due ricevitori		
Tasto ripetizione		

SWATCH TWINTAM NON SOLO DUE RICEVITORI.

MA ANCHE UNA SEGRETERIA TELEFONICA.

THE ART OF CHANGING

SEGNALI DI FUMO.

SEGNALI D'ORIENTE.

SEGNALI DI MARE.

SEGNALI DI FESTA.

SEGNALI DI SWATCH.

DA VICINO, TWINTAM, IL MASSIMO DELLA COMODITÀ: DUE RICEVITORI, MEMORIA PER VENTI NUMERI CON SELEZIONE ALFANUMERICA, TASTO DI RIPETIZIONE E TASTO FLASH. DA LONTANO, TWINTAM, IL MASSIMO DELLA PRATICITÀ: SEGRETERIA CON

RICHIAMO A DISTANZA (PER ASCOLTARE OVUNQUE I MESSAGGI RICEVUTI). E POICHÉ, OLTRE ALL'ORECCHIO, ANCHE L'OCCHIO VUOLE LA SUA PARTE, TWINTAM, LA SEGRETERIA TELEFONICA CON DUE RICEVITORI È DISPONIBILE IN TRE COLORI.

Blu, verde, rosso trasparente o grigio. Design Swatch fuori, alta tecnologia dentro. Batteria ecologica senza effetto memoria. Lire 840.000+IVA.

NUMERO VERDE 1678-21014

swatch cellular

DUE TELEFONI — UNA SEGRETERIA TELEFONICA.

DIALOGO 3 | *Verifichiamo!*

Michael e Simonetta cercano* di risolvere il problema. (*cercare)

Michael and Simonetta try to solve the problem.

Studiate queste espressioni, ascoltatele e ripetetele nelle pause previste.

hai* ragione (avere)	*you are right*
sullo schermo	*on screen*
verifichiamo* (verificare)	*let's check*
finalmente	*at last*

 Adesso chiudete il libro e ascoltate il dialogo.

SIMONETTA GIORGI: Vediamo . . . Hai ragione, il nome non è sullo schermo. Verifichiamo l'indice.
MICHAEL MOOR: Ecco il nome.
SIMONETTA GIORGI: Ma non è Ollimondi . . . il cliente è Arrimondi! Tommaso ha una scrittura illeggibile!
MICHAEL MOOR: Come si scrive?
SIMONETTA GIORGI: A–R–R–I–M–O–N–D–I.
MICHAEL MOOR: Ecco, finalmente! Ma qui è Arimondi, con una 'erre' sola. Adesso bisogna modificare il nome e salvare.

Ascoltate il dialogo di nuovo, questa volta con il libro aperto. Usate il tasto pausa e ripetete ogni frase.

ESERCIZIO 3.1

Choose a role and practise the dialogue with a partner. Move on to another partner and practise the same role. When you feel sure of it, change roles. Repeat the process as many times as you need.

ESERCIZIO 3.2

A colleague rings up and asks you to enter the names of three new clients on to the database. Listen carefully and key in the names. If you need to revise the alphabet go back to *Capitolo 4* before attempting this task.

ESERCIZIO 3.3

Work with a partner. You are checking the names of new clients from two different lists before entering them in the database. Read out the names from your list in turn and check that there are no mistakes or repetitions.

Modello Stimolo: Sartorini Marco, come si scrive?
Risposta: S–A–R–T–O–R–I–N–I M–A–R–C–O

Lista 1	Lista 2
Conte Roberto	De Magris Piero
Galli Federico	De Giorgi Maddalena
Magris Veronica	Ferri Marisa
Ferri Maurizio	Santori Oscar

ESERCIZIO 3.4

Do you know the Italian names for all the countries in the European Union? Match the country with the correct nationality disc, then check your answers with a partner if you wish.

Belgio
Olanda
Lussemburgo
Germania
Portogallo
Spagna
Francia
Danimarca
Gran Bretagna
Irlanda
Italia
Grecia
Finlandia
Svezia
Austria

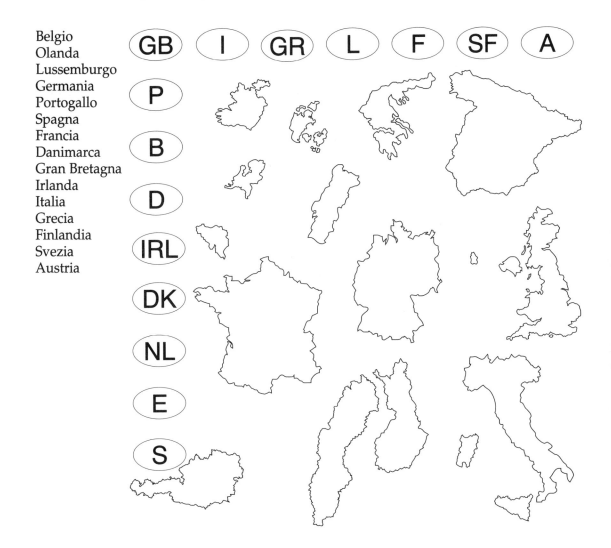

GRAMMATICA   Making comparisons in Italian is quite straightforward. Look at the statements below and see if you can work out the pattern.

la Grecia è **più** grande **del** Lussemburgo
la Francia è **meno** popolata **della** Germania
l'Italia è industriale **come** la Francia

più .... **di** ....   → more .... than . . .
meno .... **di** ....   → less .... than . . .
come ....   → as .... as . . .

ESERCIZIO 3.5

You have received some statistical data produced by the sales office. Study it carefully.

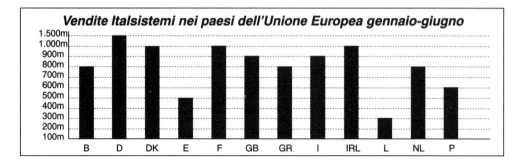

Now check whether the following statements in the Italsistemi Press Release, which is due to be published soon, are correct.

1 La Francia acquista più del Portogallo.
2 Le vendite in Belgio sono soltanto a 500 milioni.
3 La Gran Bretagna spende come la Danimarca.
4 Le vendite in Grecia sono già a seicento milioni.
5 Il Portogallo acquista meno mobili della Danimarca.

ESERCIZIO 3.6

The sales projections for October need to be entered in the database. Listen to the message Simonetta has left on the answerphone and complete the chart.

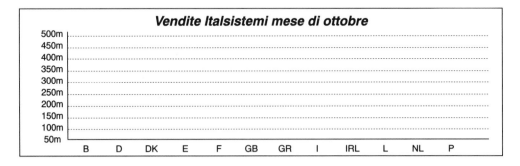

ESERCIZIO 3.7

Look again how comparisons are made in Italian in the *Grammatica* p. 103. Listen to the prompts on cassette. An agent is asking for information on sales projections. How do you respond?

Modello Stimolo: Quali sono le proiezioni di vendita per il Belgio in rapporto alla Francia?

Risposta: Secondo le proiezioni, il Belgio acquista per 120 milioni meno della Francia.

ESERCIZIO 3.8

With a partner, compare the countries below using the adjectives in the box. Remember that some countries are feminine and some are masculine, but towns are always feminine.

Modello L'Italia è più grande del Belgio.

1 la Francia	il Lussemburgo
2 il Portogallo	l'Irlanda
3 la Grecia	l'Italia
4 il Belgio	la Spagna
5 l'Olanda	la Germania
6 la Danimarca	la Grecia
7 Manchester	Londra

grande	agricolo	turistico	industriale
piccolo	caro	popolato	

ESERCIZIO 3.9

Work with a partner or in a small group. Go back to *Esercizio 2.10* (p. 100) and study the adverts again. Then, compare the merits of the two cellular phones. The adjectives below may be useful.

comodo	economico	colorato	pratico
compatto	veloce	ecologico	

DIALOGO 4 *Posso essere utile?*

Michael sente* bussare alla porta. (*sentire)

Michael hears a knock at the door.

Studiate queste espressioni, ascoltatele e ripetetele nelle pause previste.

posso* essere utile? (potere)	*can I be of help?*
in riunione	*in a meeting*
ritirare	*to pick up*
forse	*perhaps*
che seccatura!	*what a nuisance!*
vuole* scrivere (volere)	*would you like to write*

Adesso chiudete il libro e ascoltate il dialogo.

MICHAEL MOOR: Avanti!
VISITATORE: Scusi, cerco il signor Fiore.
MICHAEL MOOR: Il signor Fiore è in riunione fino alle 12.30. Posso essere utile?
VISITATORE: Devo ritirare dei programmi. Forse sono sulla sua scrivania . . . ?
MICHAEL MOOR: Vediamo . . . no, non sono qui. Forse sono nell' ufficio accanto, ma è chiuso, mi dispiace.
VISITATORE: Che seccatura!
MICHAEL MOOR: Vuole scrivere qui il suo nome e lasciare un messaggio?

Ascoltate il dialogo di nuovo, questa volta con il libro aperto. Usate il tasto pausa e ripetete ogni frase.

ESERCIZIO 4.1

Choose a role and practise the dialogue with a partner. Move on to another partner and practise the same role. When you feel sure of it, change roles. Repeat the process as many times as you need.

ESERCIZIO 4.2

Listen to the dialogue again and answer the following questions.

1 Where is Tommaso Fiore?
2 Why has the visitor come to the office?
3 Why is Michael unable to give the visitor what he's looking for?
4 What suggestion does Michael make?

ESERCIZIO 4.3

The visitor leaves a message for Tommaso Fiore. What does it say?

```
      M E S S A G G I
Per          Tommaso Fiore
Da parte di  Corrado Nolla

Testo        Telefono prima di
       domani
       Sono in ufficio fino alle 19.
       Devo avere i programmi
       urgentemente.


Data  3/11    Firma    Corrado
```

ESERCIZIO 4.4

What a day! The telephone rings. It is a client and he wishes to speak with
Tommaso Fiore. Be as helpful as possible. There are a number of possible
responses for you to choose from.

AGENTE: Pronto? Vorrei parlare con il signor Fiore, per favore.
LEI: *I am sorry, Mr Fiore is not here/in the office.*
AGENTE: E dov'è?
LEI: *He is in a meeting/with the sales manager/in reception/with the agents/in Milan.*
AGENTE: Che seccatura!
LEI: *Would you like to leave a message/ring tomorrow/speak with the secretary?*
AGENTE: Grazie, lascio un messaggio. Dunque . . . è pronto a scrivere?

ESERCIZIO 4.5

Now take down the message from the agent. Make sure you write his name
correctly.

```
      M E S S A G G I
Per          ----------------------
Da parte di  ----------------------

Testo        ----------------------
       ----------------------------
       ----------------------------
       ----------------------------
       ----------------------------
       ----------------------------
       ----------------------------
       ----------------------------

Data ----------  Firma ------------
```

ESERCIZIO 4.6

Before you return to work after the interruptions you decide to have a look at the newspaper. What are today's headlines?

1 **La Gran Bretagna al primo posto nel campionato di tennis**

3 **La nuova generazione musicale al festival di Glastonbury in Inghilterra.**

2 *Fine della recessione in Europa?*

4 *Fine di un mito: L'Ungheria esporta più vino dell'Italia?*

5 **Dieci scienziati italiani in un incidente aereo nelle Alpi francesi**

6 **TERRORE A NUOVA YORK: DUE COCCODRILLI SPARITI DALLO ZOO**

7 **Domani in città sciopero della metropolitana : tutti in bicicletta?**

Which article deals with:

a A local strike?   **d** The economy?   **g** Exports?
b A sports event?   **e** A missing animal?
c An air crash?   **f** Rock and pop music?

ESERCIZIO 4.7

Che seccatura! You really need to know the digital lock code to get into the adjoining office. Find a colleague, explain the problem and ask for the combination. You may use the guidelines opposite if you wish to structure your conversation.

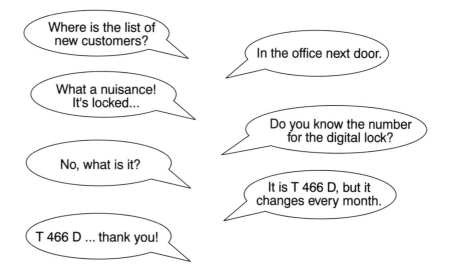

DA NOTARE You have now learned how to express annoyance (*che seccatura!*). Here are a few more expressions you can use.

che bello!   *how lovely!*
che simpatico!   *what a charming person!*
che noia!   *how boring!*
che confusione!   *what a mess!*

ESERCIZIO 4.8

Work with a partner or in a small group. Look at the pictures below and for each one give your reaction.

Prima di continuare

Before going on to Chapter 6, make sure that you can:

• ask if someone can operate the database	*sa usare la banca dati?*
• confirm that you can	*credo di sì*
• explain what must be done	*bisogna . . .*
• ask about the password	*che password usate?*
• check if the printer is switched on	*la stampante è accesa?*
• say that you are going now	*ora vado*
• ask a colleague to do something for you	*mi può/puoi . . . ?*
• say that there is a problem	*c'è un problema*
• explain what the problem is	*devo . . . ma non trovo/funziona . . .*
• suggest checking something over	*verifichiamo*
• ask how a word is spelt	*come si scrive . . . ?*
• make a comparison	*è più/meno . . . di . . . come . . .*
• offer assistance	*posso essere utile?*
• express regret	*mi dispiace*
• make a suggestion	*vuole (lasciare un messaggio) . . . ?*

Fuori ufficio

In this chapter you will learn how to:
- talk about yourself and enquire about people's background
- get information about services and accommodation
- order a meal
- express your thanks

DIALOGO 1 *Cosa fai in Inghilterra?*

Michael va alla Fiera del Mobile con i colleghi.

Michael goes to the Furniture Fair with his colleagues.

Studiate queste espressioni, ascoltatele e ripetetele nelle pause previste.

frequento* un corso (frequentare)	*I am following a course*
gestione commerciale	*business management*
finanziaria	*financial*
fratelli e sorelle	*brothers and sisters*
studia lingue	*studies languages*
se vuoi* (volere)	*if you wish*
insieme	*together*
mi piacerebbe* molto (piacere)	*I would like that very much*

 Adesso chiudete il libro e ascoltate il dialogo.

COLLEGA:	Cosa fai in Inghilterra, Michael?
MICHAEL MOOR:	Frequento un corso di gestione commerciale internazionale a Londra da due anni.
COLLEGA:	È interessante?
MICHAEL MOOR:	Sì, ma il secondo anno è abbastanza difficile, soprattutto la parte finanziaria e la parte legale.
SIMONETTA GIORGI:	Hai fratelli e sorelle?
MICHAEL MOOR:	Sì, ho un fratello di diciassette anni che studia lingue a Bristol e una sorella sposata che abita a Liverpool da sei mesi. E tu, sei di Bologna?
SIMONETTA GIORGI:	Sì, sono di Bologna. Se vuoi, possiamo visitare la città insieme.
MICHAEL MOOR:	Mi piacerebbe molto, grazie.

 Ascoltate il dialogo di nuovo, questa volta con il libro aperto. Usate il tasto pausa e ripetete ogni frase.

ESERCIZIO 1.1

Choose a role and practise the dialogue with two partners. Move on to other partners and practise the same role. When you feel sure of it, change roles. Repeat the process as many times as you wish.

ESERCIZIO 1.2

Look at the map and answer the questions:

1 Dove abita il fratello di Michael?
2 Chi abita a Liverpool?
3 Dove studia Michael in Inghilterra?

GRAMMATICA   *How long have you been . . . ?*

Saying that you have been doing something for a certain length of time is quite straightforward in Italian.

frequento un corso . . . **da** due anni
(mia sorella) **abita** a Liverpool **da** sei mesi

All you have to do is to use the present tense of the verb you need and the preposition *da* before the indication of time.

Also: da aprile   *since april*
             dal 1993   *since 1993*

If you wish to ask how long someone has been doing something you say:

Da quanto tempo lavora alla Italsistemi?
Da quanto tempo abita a Bologna?

ESERCIZIO 1.3

These young people are all taking part in a national project on the protection of the environment through their creative skills. Listen to the cassette and enter the details you hear in the grid below.

Nome	è di ... (città)	abita a ... (città)	cosa fa	da quanto tempo
Daniela				
Diego				
Sabrina				
Alessandro				
Cecilia				

ESERCIZIO 1.4

Select one item from each column and make up at least three sentences.

studio	al festival rock	dal	1993
abito	l'italiano	da	età di 17 anni
ho	una moto	dall'	1992
faccio	a Plymouth		otto anni
uso	windsurf		tre mesi
vado	il computer		dieci anni

Now find a partner and listen to each other's sentences. Write them down. Move on to a different partner and repeat the process.

ESERCIZIO 1.5

You are waiting for the opening speech at a trade fair and you overhear a conversation. Listen to the cassette first then look at the text below and listen again before filling the gaps. You may need to listen to the conversation several times.

SIGNORE: No, non .... bolognese, ... di Palermo, ma .... in Centro Italia .... 1985. Mia sorella .... fisica nucleare a Torino .... due anni. E Lei, ... tempo abita a Bologna?

SIGNORA: Ora .... a Bologna .... due anni per ...., ma .... di Modena. Abito con mio fratello .... gennaio, ma cerco un appartamento .... un mese. Non è facile!

ESERCIZIO 1.6

Il lavoro di domani?

Ecco alcune professioni del futuro secondo esperti in previsioni strategiche del lavoro in Europa.

Occupazione	Posti di lavoro nel 2015
Bibliotecario informatizzato	11.000
Tecnico effetti speciali (visivi, sonori)	2.000
Esperto in turismo (arte, sport, natura)	3.500
Manager di aree protette (oasi, parchi . . .)	700
Docente in lingue straniere	4.000
Esperto in orientamento scuola-lavoro	5.500
Terapista occupazionale	7.000

Look at the information on future professions in Europe. Can you find the nearest British equivalent for each profession? Compare your findings with a partner.

GRAMMATICA   *Mi piacerebbe*

Saying that you would like to do something in Italian is quite simple. Look at the examples below:

> **mi piacerebbe** avere una moto
> **mi piacerebbe** lavorare in America

All you have to do is to use *mi piacerebbe* followed by a suitable verb from the dictionary.

You can add *abbastanza* to say that you are quite keen;
molto if you are really keen;
non mi piacerebbe if you don't want to.

If you wish to ask what someone would like to do or to invite someone to do something, you either use *ti piacerebbe . . . ?* if you are on informal terms, *Le piacerebbe* if you are not, or *vi piacerebbe* to more than one person.

Le piacerebbe lavorare in Inghilterra?	(*Michael to Tommaso*)
ti piacerebbe lavorare in Inghilterra?	(*Michael to Simonetta*)
vi piacerebbe visitare Londra?	(*Michael to both*)

ESERCIZIO 1.7

Listen to the four mini-dialogues on the cassette and find out which of the activities listed below the speakers would like to do. Record your answers with a tick.

1 andare al cinema ☐
2 andare alla partita di calcio ☐
3 visitare una fiera ☐
4 andare in discoteca ☐
5 visitare il museo ☐
6 fare una passeggiata ☐
7 guardare un film alla televisione ☐

ESERCIZIO 1.8

Le piacerebbe/ti piacerebbe/vi piacerebbe?
Invite the people below to join you in your activities:

1 visitare il museo   (un collega giovane)
2 andare al ristorante   (due colleghi)
3 visitare la fiera del computer   (un cliente)
4 andare al cinema   (un gruppo di colleghi)
5 venire alla riunione   (un agente di filiale)

ESERCIZIO 1.9

Work in a group. Ask each other questions about jobs and working patterns and note what the most popular choices are.

Modello   Domanda   Ti piacerebbe lavorare come tecnico?
              Risposta   Sì mi piacerebbe molto.

1 .... lavorare all'estero?
2 .... usare le lingue per lavoro?
3 .... diventare agente di vendita?
4 .... diventare manager?
5 .... avere un orario flessibile?
6 .... diventare esperto di turismo?
7 .... avere un lavoro part-time?
8 .... diventare segretario bilingue?
9 .... avere un lavoro indipendente?
10 .... lavorare in un ufficio?
11 .... lavorare in un negozio?
12 .... lavorare come direttore vendite?

DA NOTARE *La scuola in Italia*

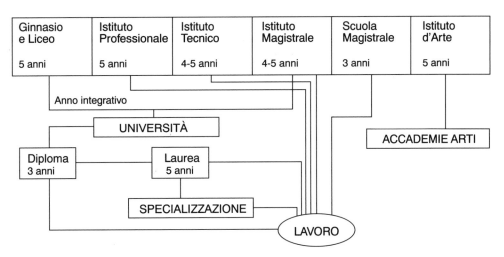

In Italia la scuola è obbligatoria dai sei ai quattordici anni (in futuro fino ai sedici anni dopo la riforma del sistema). Dai tre ai cinque anni è possibile frequentare la scuola dell'infanzia. Dai sei ai dieci anni i bambini frequentano la scuola elementare e dagli undici ai quattordici anni la scuola media unica. Dopo la scuola media unica, i giovani possono scegliere secondo le preferenze, come mostra il grafico.

ESERCIZIO 1.10

Look at the information on the Italian education system and answer the questions:

1 Cosa può frequentare un bambino a quattro anni?
2 Cosa frequenta un giovane a tredici anni?
3 Cosa si può fare dopo l'istituto professionale?
4 Dove può andare uno studente con talento artistico?
5 Cosa si può fare dopo la laurea?

ESERCIZIO 1.11

Two business people ask about each other's family. Naturally they are pleased to talk about their children and how they are getting on in school. Listen to the cassette and study the grid below. Then listen to the cassette as many times as you need in order to enter the details in the grid.

Nome	Età	Frequenta	Preferisce	Problemi
Ferruccio				
Alba				
Paoletta				
Maria				
Franco				

DA NOTARE   *Come va?*

Showing some interest in a colleague's personal background is a sign of courtesy in Italy. Here are a few useful expressions to keep the conversation flowing. Remember what Simonetta asks Michael in *Dialogo 1: Hai fratelli e sorelle?* Here are a few more:

come va la famiglia?	*how is the family?*
tuo fratello ha figli?	*has your brother got children?*
che scuola frequentano?	*what school do they attend?*
che lavoro fa tua sorella?	*what job does your sister do?*

ESERCIZIO 1.12

Work in pairs. Practise finding out about your partner's background. The guidelines below are intended to help you structure your conversation but you do not need to restrict yourself to them.

Are you from ... (town)?

No, I am from ..... but I have been living here for six years

Have you got brothers and sisters?

Yes, two sisters. One works in Glasgow and lives with a friend and the other is on work experience in Manchester

How long have you been doing work experience?

For a week only

Is it interesting?

Oh yes, but the financial side is difficult

What do you study in England?

I study business management

.... and languages?

Yes, I have been studying Italian and German for a year. It is difficult but very interesting

You speak Italian well!

Oh...thanks...but I do not understand everything...

DIALOGO 2 *Soldi!*

Michael deve andare in banca.

Michael must go to the bank.

 Studiate queste espressioni, ascoltatele e ripetetele nelle pause previste.

andare in banca	*to go to the bank*
la carta di credito	*the credit card*
prelevare i soldi	*to withdraw money*
Bancomat	*bank cash dispenser*
sei molto organizzato!	*you are very organised!*

 Adesso chiudete il libro e ascoltate il dialogo.

MICHAEL MOOR: Domani devo andare in banca. Le banche aprono alle 9, vero?

SIMONETTA GIORGI: No, più presto, alle 8.30.

MICHAEL MOOR: Grazie. Vorrei cambiare i travellers.

SIMONETTA GIORGI: Se hai la carta di credito, puoi prelevare i soldi direttamente dal Bancomat.

MICHAEL MOOR: Sì, è vero, ma è più caro, devo pagare gli interessi alla banca!

SIMONETTA GIORGI: Sei molto organizzato!

 Ascoltate il dialogo di nuovo, questa volta con il libro aperto. Usate il tasto pausa e ripetete ogni frase.

ESERCIZIO 2.1

Choose a role and practise the dialogue with a partner. Move on to a different partner and practise the same role. When you feel sure of it, change roles. Repeat the process as many times as you need.

DA NOTARE   *Orari di apertura*

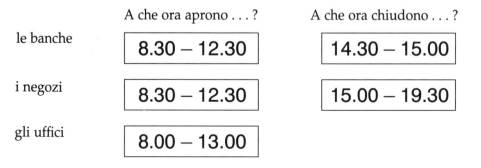

	A che ora aprono . . . ?	A che ora chiudono . . . ?
le banche	8.30 – 12.30	14.30 – 15.00
i negozi	8.30 – 12.30	15.00 – 19.30
gli uffici	8.00 – 13.00	

Negozi e grandi magazzini hanno mezza giornata di chiusura. Gli orari possono variare a seconda delle città.

ESERCIZIO 2.2

Listen to the recorded message left on the answerphone of the town Tourist Office and complete the grid below.

	aprono	chiudono	giornata di apertura
Grandi magazzini			
Cinema			
Discoteche			
Ristoranti			
Negozi			
Uffici pubblici			

ESERCIZIO 2.3

When you wish to say 'they', take off the endings of the verb (*–are*, *–ere*, or *–ire*) and add the appropriate endings. See p. 79.

Look at the pictures and complete the captions with the correct form of a suitable verb from the list below.

guardare	partire	finire	prendere
visitare	usare	mangiare	ballare

Cosa fanno?

1 .... in treno
2 .... al ristorante
3 .... un cognac e una birra
4 .... i computer

5 .... in discoteca
6 .... un museo
7 .... un film

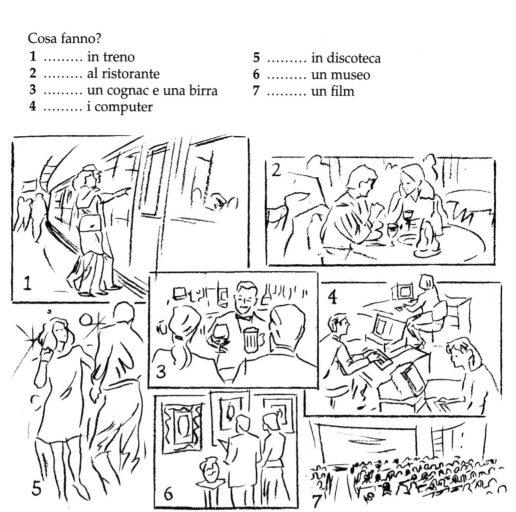

ESERCIZIO 2.4

Study the exchange rates then answer the questions.

1 How many German marks would you get for 200.000 Italian lire?
2 What would you get in UK pounds for 100.000 Italian lire?
3 You change 50.000 Italian lire into French francs: how much do you get?

MERCATO VALUTARIO		
Cambi	In lire	C/dollaro
Dollaro Usa	1.629,620	–
Ecu	1.881,230	1,1544
Marco tedesco	977,230	1,6676
Franco francese	285,650	5,7050
Lira sterlina	2.436,610	1,4952
Fiorino olandese	868,990	1,8753
Franco belga	47,438	34,3526

ESERCIZIO 2.5

Now, in pairs, convert all the currencies below into Italian lire.

1 Lira Sterlina   100
2 Franco francese   5.000
3 Dollaro USA   16.000
4 Marco tedesco   10.000

ESERCIZIO 2.6

Michael is trying to change some money but he is not sure he understands what the bank clerk is telling him. Can you help him? Listen to the cassette and provide the missing part.

MICHAEL MOOR: Vorrei cambiare dei travellers', per favore.
IMPIEGATO: Quanto vuole cambiare?
MICHAEL MOOR: ………
IMPIEGATO: Il cambio della sterlina inglese è ……… quindi sono ………
                lire. Ha un documento?
MICHAEL MOOR: Sì. Scusi, ma il cambio di oggi non è ……… lire per sterlina?
IMPIEGATO: Sì, ma c'è una tariffa di ……… lire per il servizio bancario.

GRAMMATICA   I wish to . . .

To say politely that you wish to do something you can use *vorrei* followed by a suitable verb from the dictionary.

vorrei cambiare i travellers'

ESERCIZIO 2.7

Tell your colleagues what you would like to do in the office today, using any combination of verbs and pictures below.

Modello   Vorrei usare la fotocopiatrice.

mandare	prendere	archiviare	stampare
controllare	telefonare	noleggiare	usare

ESERCIZIO 2.8

Finding accommodation in Italian cities can be difficult and expensive but not impossible.

ANNUNCIO
Affitto bella e grande camera con cucina e servizi in comune in appartamento in centro città a dieci minuti dall'Università. Disponibile subito. Solo studenti o giovani lavoratori. Referenze indispensabili. Lire 420mila mensili tutto compreso.
Telefonare al (051) 98 44 67 la mattina o dopo le ore 20.

Study the advert then answer the questions. You may need to consult the Glossary but try and make a guess before you do.

1 What is offered for rent?
2 Where is the apartment situated?
3 What kind of people is the advert trying to attract?
4 What would you need to supply if you wished to rent it?
5 Does the monthly rent include all expenses?

ESERCIZIO 2.9

Work with a partner. You are both interested in the accommodation but before you ring you need to practise giving information about yourselves. Follow the guidelines below to play in turn the roles of the enquirer and the proprietor.

- Hello? My name is ... You are letting a room?
- Good morning. Yes, a nice room in the apartment.
- Is it available immediately?
- Yes. Are you a student?
- Yes, I am a student from London. I am here on work experience at the Tronchetti company.
- How long have you been in Bologna?
- I have been here for five days only, but I would like to work in Bologna from April to November.
- You speak Italian well!
- Thank you! I have been studying Italian for six months.
- Can you come and see the room today?
- Yes, when I finish work at 6 p.m. The address is...?
- Via Oberdeen 159. The name is Bortdoni.

DIALOGO 3 *Cosa facciamo stasera?*

Michael passa una serata con i colleghi.

Michael spends an evening with his colleagues.

Studiate queste espressioni, ascoltatele e ripetetele nelle pause previste.

se non sei stanco	*if you are not tired*
vieni* ... con noi (venire)	*come ... with us*
passiamo* dal tuo albergo (passare)	*we'll call at your hotel*
molta scelta	*a lot of choice*
se hai molta fame	*if you are very hungry*
un antipasto	*a starter*
un primo	*a first course*
un secondo	*a main course*
e da bere?	*and to drink?*
un brindisi	*a toast*

 Adesso chiudete il libro e ascoltate il dialogo.

SIMONETTA GIORGI: Se non sei stanco, Michael, vieni anche tu al ristorante con noi. Celebriamo la promozione di Tommaso. Passiamo dal tuo albergo alle 20. Va bene?

MICHAEL MOOR: D'accordo, volentieri.

Al ristorante

CAMERIERE: E per Lei?

MICHAEL MOOR: Non so ... c'è molta scelta ...

SIMONETTA GIORGI: Se hai molta fame prendi un antipasto, un primo e un secondo. Se no, solo un secondo.

MICHAEL MOOR: Allora prendo solo un secondo, il pollo arrosto con patatine fritte e insalata mista.

CAMERIERE: ... e da bere?

TOMMASO FIORE: Vino rosso e acqua minerale per tutti?

TUTTI: Sì, d'accordo, va bene.

SIMONETTA GIORGI: Allora, un brindisi per la promozione di Tommaso. Congratulazioni!

TUTTI: Congratulazioni Tommaso!

Ascoltate il dialogo di nuovo, questa volta con il libro aperto. Usate il tasto pausa e ripetete ogni frase.

ESERCIZIO 3.1

Choose a role and practise the dialogue with a partner. Move on to a different partner and practise the same role. When you feel sure of it, change roles. Repeat the process as many times as you need.

ESERCIZIO 3.2

Study the menu and answer the questions. You may have to look up some words in the Glossary.

Menu

Antipasti
Prosciutto con melone
Pomodori ripieni

Primi piatti
Lasagne
Risotto alla milanese
Minestrone

Secondi piatti
Pollo arrosto
Bistecca alla fiorentina
Torta di verdure
Salmone scozzese

Contorni
Palatine
Insalata mista
Spinaci

Formaggi Dolci

1 Sei vegetariano: cosa prendi di secondo?
2 Preferisci non mangiare pesce: cosa puoi mangiare?
3 In un ristorante italiano si serve prima il dolce o il formaggio?

ESERCIZIO 3.3

Michael's colleagues are ready to order. Listen to what each of them has chosen. Listen to the conversation as many times as you need to complete the grid below.

Piatti	Simonetta	Tommaso	Daniela
Prosciutto con melone			
Pomodori ripieni			
Lasagne			
Risotto alla milanese			
Minestrone			
Pollo arrosto			
Bistecca alla fiorentina			
Torta di verdure			
Salmone scozzese			
Patatine fritte			
Insalata mista			
Spinaci			

ESERCIZIO 3.4

Work with a partner. Ask what s/he would choose from the menu above and say what your choice would be. Move on to a different partner and repeat the process. As a group, you can now work out what the most popular choice is.

DA NOTARE   *Cosa facciamo?*

Making and responding to suggestions can be done quite simply. Look at the examples below:

Cosa facciamo?

Proposte	Risposte
si può . . .	sì, volentieri
possiamo . . .	sì, per me va bene
se volete . . .	mi piacerebbe molto
preferisci . . .	preferisco . . .

ESERCIZIO 3.5

Michael and his colleagues make plans for the rest of the evening. Listen to the cassette first then study the suggestions below and listen again to the conversation until you are certain of what has been agreed and in which order.

1 andare al cinema
2 andare in discoteca
3 andare in gelateria
4 andare da Simonetta
5 fare una passeggiata in centro
6 andare al karaoke

ESERCIZIO 3.6

Quanto costa uscire la sera?

6.000 lire	un ingresso al cinema
3.500 lire	una birra
7.000 lire	una pizza
15.000 lire	un ingresso in discoteca
3.000 lire	un gelato
40.000 lire	un ingresso al concerto

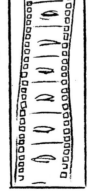

Vero   Falso

1 Un gelato è più caro di una birra.
2 Un concerto rock è meno caro della discoteca.
3 Due birre costano come una pizza.
4 Il cinema è meno caro della discoteca.

Study the adverts then make a suggestion for an evening out for each of the following people.

1 a karaoke devotee
2 a beer connoisseur
3 a skating enthusiast
4 a theatre lover
5 a rock fan

ESERCIZIO 3.8

Work with a partner. Look at the adverts in *Esercizio 3.7* again, consider the cost, then agree on how to spend an evening. When you have agreed, move on to another set of partners and try to persuade them to join you for the evening.

DIALOGO 4 *Grazie per il suo aiuto!*

È l'ultimo giorno alla Italsistemi. Michael ringrazia e saluta i colleghi.

It is the last day at Italsistemi. Michael thanks his colleagues and says goodbye.

Studiate queste espressioni, ascoltatele e ripetetele nelle pause previste.

cosa pensa* di (pensare)	*what do you think about . . .*
molto utile	*very useful*
non so come ringraziare	*I don't know how to thank you*
non c'è di che	*don't mention it*
è un vero piacere	*it is a real pleasure*
complimenti	*congratulations*
auguri per gli studi	*best wishes for your studies*
un piccolo omaggio	*a small gift*

Adesso chiudete il libro e ascoltate il dialogo.

MATTEO CERULLI:	Allora, Michael, cosa pensa di questa esperienza di lavoro?
MICHAEL MOOR:	Molto utile, davvero. Non so come ringraziare per tutto.
SIMONETTA GIORGI:	Non c'è di che. È un vero piacere per noi.
MICHAEL MOOR:	Siete molto gentili. Arrivederci signor Fiore, grazie per il suo aiuto. Adesso so come funziona un'agenda elettronica!
TOMMASO FIORE:	Ora Lei è un vero esperto di informatica . . . e complimenti anche per l'italiano! Arrivederci a presto, forse in Inghilterra . . .
MATTEO CERULLI:	Arrivederci, Michael, e auguri per gli studi. Questo è un piccolo omaggio della Italsistemi . . .
MICHAEL MOOR:	Oh, un libro su Bologna . . . grazie, dottor Cerulli! Arrivederci, Simonetta e grazie per tutto!
SIMONETTA GIORGI:	Ciao, Michael, buon viaggio e non dimenticare di scrivere!
COLLEGHI:	Ciao Michael, arrivederci!

Ascoltate il dialogo di nuovo, questa volta con il libro aperto. Usate il tasto pausa e ripetete ogni frase.

ESERCIZIO 4.1

Choose a role and practise the dialogue with three partners. Change roles and repeat the process until you all feel confident that you really know the dialogue.

ESERCIZIO 4.2

Preferisce, preferisci o preferisco?

SIMONETTA GIORGI:	Michael, ... andare all'aeroporto in bus o in taxi?
MICHAEL MOOR:	Grazie, ... prendere il bus.
MATTEO CERULLI:	Cosa .... fare per la sua ultima giornata a Bologna, Michael?
TOMMASO FIORE:	Sono sicuro che Michael .... visitare i musei.
SIMONETTA GIORGI:	Ma forse Michael .... comprare dei regali per la famiglia e gli amici in Inghilterra. Chiediamo a Michael. Cosa .... fare, esattamente?

ESERCIZIO 4.3

Look at the *Standa* advert. It advertises a service open to all customers of this well-known chain store (*grande magazzino*).

1 In what way does this service help the customer?
2 Where is it available?

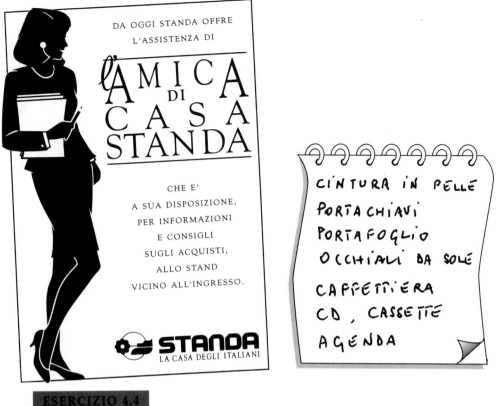

DA OGGI STANDA OFFRE
L'ASSISTENZA DI

l'AMICA DI CASA STANDA

CHE E'
A SUA DISPOSIZIONE,
PER INFORMAZIONI
E CONSIGLI
SUGLI ACQUISTI,
ALLO STAND
VICINO ALL'INGRESSO.

STANDA
LA CASA DEGLI ITALIANI

CINTURA IN PELLE
PORTA CHIAVI
PORTAFOGLIO
OCCHIALI DA SOLE
CAFFETTIERA
CD, CASSETTE
AGENDA

ESERCIZIO 4.4

Michael is looking for some presents to take back to England. Simonetta has jotted down a list of items. What does she suggest?

ESERCIZIO 4.5

Where in the store would Michael find the presents on the list? Look at the noticeboard at the store entrance.

Benvenuti alla Standa

Piano terreno

Profumeria e cosmetici
Libri e musica
Oggetti regalo
Oggetti di cartoleria

Secondo piano

Tutto per la casa
Tutto per il giardino
Tutto per il viaggio

Primo piano

Abbigliamento donna e uomo
Accessori
Abbigliamento bambini

Terzo piano

Mobili e tappeti
Bar - Telefoni
Toelette
Parrucchiere
Servizio clienti

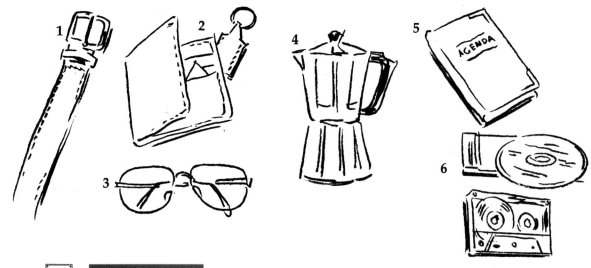

ESERCIZIO 4.6

You visit the *Standa* store on the day they are launching the customer service advertised above. Nothing is where it should be! Find the customer service staff (*l'Amica di Casa Standa*) and explain what you want by listening to the cassette and responding as suggested.

ESERCIZIO 4.7

Work with a partner and practise the dialogue, following the guidelines to structure your conversation if you wish and exchanging roles. You can now probably use the language more freely and confidently, so do not let the guidelines limit you. Be bold and try and use as much language as you can.

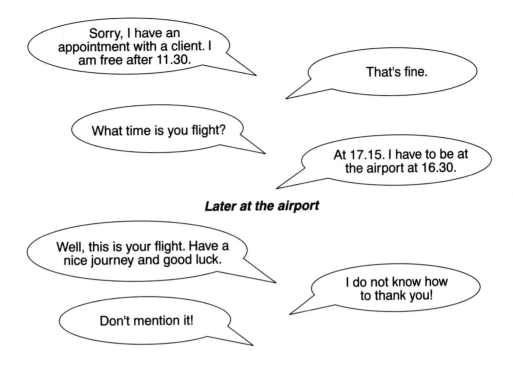

Sorry, I have an appointment with a client. I am free after 11.30.

That's fine.

What time is you flight?

At 17.15. I have to be at the airport at 16.30.

Later at the airport

Well, this is your flight. Have a nice journey and good luck.

I do not know how to thank you!

Don't mention it!

ESERCIZIO 4.8

Back in England, Michael has just received a letter from Simonetta.

What does she say about:

1 Tommaso?
2 Her work plans?
3 Her accommodation?

13 Aprile

Caro Michael

Come stai? Spero tutto bene. Qui alla Italsistemi è la solita vita – c'è molto lavoro ma, come sai, lavoriamo bene insieme.

Tommaso è in Germania per due settimane e manda almeno cinque fax al giorno!

Per il momento io lavoro all'ufficio Servizio Clienti. A giugno faccio un corso di gestione commerciale internazionale a Roma.

Ora abito in un nuovo appartamento vicino all'università da tre settimane e sono molto contenta. È piccolo ma non è troppo caro.

Tutti i colleghi mandano saluti e auguri per gli esami.

Scrivi presto! Cari saluti.

Simonetta

DA NOTARE   You need to take some care when addressing people and organisations in writing. Look at the examples below:

Lettera personale   Lettera commerciale

ESERCIZIO 4.9

Write a short letter to Simonetta, asking her news, giving her news about your studies and your plans.

Now you have completed Capitolo sei, you are ready to move on to *Hotel Europa Italia. Congratulazioni!*

Before you do, make sure you can:

• say how long you have being doing something	*abito a Londra da due anni*
• ask someone how long they have been doing something	*da quanto tempo lavora . . . ?*
• talk about your studies	*frequento un corso di . . .*
• ask about a colleague's family	*che lavoro fa tua sorella?*
• say what you would like to do	*mi piacerebbe lavorare . . .*
• ask what people would like to do	*Le piacerebbe . . . ?*
• enquire about opening hours	*a che ora aprono le banche?*
• carry out a bank transaction	*vorrei cambiare i travellers'*
• make suggestions	*se volete, si può andare . . .*
• respond to suggestions	*preferisco andare . . .*
• plan an evening out with friends	*cosa facciamo stasera*
• ask someone's opinion	*cosa pensi di . . . ?*
• say how grateful you are	*non so come ringraziare*
• say goodbye	*arrivederci, non dimenticare di scrivere!*

GLOSSARY

Nouns are indicated as (n) and genders are given: m = masculine, f = feminine. They are given in the singular and plural forms where the plural is irregular, e.g. *albergo, alberghi*. Where only a plural form is given, it is indicated (mpl) or (fpl). For more information about nouns see pages 11 and 37.

Verbs are marked with an asterisk and a page reference number is given to check on how to use them. Irregular verbs are given in full.

Adjectives are indicated as (adj) and are given with the masculine singular ending, followed by the feminine singular, masculine plural and feminine plural endings for adjectives with four forms, e.g. *bravo/a/i/e*, and the singular and plural forms for adjectives which have two forms, e.g. *accidentale/i*. For more information on adjectives see page 31.

Note: the translations given here are those most appropriate in the context of the dialogues and exercises. In many cases, other meanings are possible.

a, (al, all', allo, alla)   *at, to*
abbastanza   *quite, enough*
abbigliamento (n) (m)   *ladies- and menswear*
abitare*   *to live (see p. 79)*
abrasione (n) (f)   *abrasion, scratching*
accanto   *next to*
accendere*   *to switch on, to light (see p. 79)*
acceso/a/i/e (adj)   *switched on*
accessori (n) (mpl)   *accessories*
accidentale/i (adj)   *accidental*
accompagnare*   *to accompany (see p. 79)*
acqua minerale (n) (f)   *mineral water*
acquistare*   *to buy (see p. 79)*
acquisti (n) (mpl)   *purchases*
aereo (n) (m)   *plane*
   in aereo   *by plane*
aeroporto (n) (m)   *airport*
affare (n) (m)   *business, deal*
affittare*   *to rent (see p. 79)*
agenda (n) (f)   *diary/filofax*
agente (n) (m)   *agent*
agenzia (n) (f)   *agency*
agricolo/a/i/e (adj)   *agricultural*
aiutare*   *to help (see p. 79)*
albergo, alberghi (n) (m)   *hotel(s)*
alfabetico/a (adj)   *alphabetical*
alfabeto (n) (m)   *alphabet*
allora   *then, so*
almeno   *at least*
Alpi (n) (fpl)   *Alps*
altro/a   *other*
amico, amica, amici, amiche (n) (m, f, pl)   *friends*
anche   *too, also*
   anche tu   *you too*
   anch'io   *me to*
andare* vado, vai, va, andiamo, andate, vanno   *to go*
andato   *gone*
   è andato*   *went*
anno (n) (m)   *year*
antipasto (n) (m)   *starter*
apertura (n) (f)   *opening*
apparecchio (n) (m)   *machine*
appartamento (n) (m)   *flat, apartment*
appuntamento (n) (m)   *appointment*
aprire*   *to open (see p. 79)*
aranciata (n) (f)   *orangeade*
architetto (n) (m)   *architect*
archiviare*   *to file (see p. 79)*

archivio (n) (m)   *file*
arrivare*   *to arrive (see p. 79)*
arrivederci   *goodbye*
arrivo (n) (m)   *arrival*
ascensore (n) (m)   *lift*
ascoltare*   *to listen to (see p. 79)*
aspettare*   *to wait (for) (see p. 79)*
assistente personale (n) (m/f)   *personal assistant*
attimo (n) (m)   *moment*
auguri (n) (mpl)   *(good) wishes*
auto (n) (f)   *car*
autobus (n) (m)   *bus*
avanti   *come in, come forward*
avere*: ho, hai, ha, abbiamo, avete, hanno   *to have*
avere appetito   *to be hungry*
avere ragione   *to be right*
azzurro/a/i/e (adj)   *blue*

bagno (n)(m)   *bath*
ballare*   *to dance (see p. 79)*
bambino/a (n) (m/f)   *child*
banca/banche (n) (f)   *bank*
banca dati (n) (f)   *database*
Bancomat   *bank cash dispenser*
bar (n) (m)   *café, bar*
barra (n) (f) spaziatrice   *space bar*
basta*   *it's enough, sufficient to (see p. 76)*
batteria (n) (f)   *battery*
bello/a/e/i (adj)   *beautiful, handsome, lovely, nice*
benvenuto/a/i/e (adj)   *welcome*
bene   *well*
bere*   *to drink*
bianco/a/chi/che (adj)   *white*
bibliotecario (n) (m)   *librarian*
bicicletta (n) (f)   *bicycle*
biglietto (n) (m)   *ticket*
bilingue/i (adj)   *bilingual*
birra (n) (f)   *beer*
bisogna*   *it is necessary, one needs to (see p. 76)*
bistecca (n) (f) alla fiorentina   *grilled T-bone steak*
bloc-notes (n) (m)   *notepad*
blocchetto (n) (m)   *block of tickets*
brindisi (n) (m)   *toast*
buonasera   *good evening*
buongiorno   *good morning*
bussare*   *to knock (see p. 79)*

c'è*   *there is*
cabine telefoniche (n) (fpl)   *telephone kiosks*
caffè (n) (m)   *coffee*
calcio (n) (m)   *football*
cambiare*   *to change (see p. 79)*
cambio (n) (m)   *change*
camera (n) (f)   *room*
cameriere (n) (m)   *waiter*
campionato (n) (m)   *championship*
cancellare*   *to delete (computer) (see p. 79)*
cancellazione (n) (f)   *deletion (computer)*
capire*   *to understand (see p. 79)*
   ho capito*   *I've understood*
caro/a/i/e (adj)   *expensive*
carta (n) (f)   *paper*
   carta (n) (f) di credito   *credit card*
cartoleria (n) (f)   *stationery*
casa (n) (f)   *home, house*
cassa (n) (f)   *cash desk*
cassetto (n) (m)   *drawer*
c'è   *there is*
   ci sono*   *there are*
celebrare*   *to celebrate (see p. 79)*
centro (n) (m)   *centre*
cercare*: cerco, cerchi, cerca, cerchiamo, cercate, cercano   *to look for*
certo   *certainly*
che?   *what?*
   che cosa?   *what?*
che   *that, who*
chi?   *who?*
chiave (n) (f)   *key*
chiedere*   *to ask (for) (see p. 79)*
chilometro (n) (m)   *kilometres*
chiudere*   *to close (see p. 79)*
chiuso/a/i/e (adj)   *closed, shut*
chiusura (n) (f)   *closing*
ciao   *hello*
circa   *about*
città (n) (f)   *town*
cliente (n) (m/f)   *client, customer*
coccodrillo (n) (m)   *crocodile*
codice (n) (m)   *code*
cognac (n) (m)   *brandy*
cognome (n) (m)   *surname*
collega (n) (m/f)   *colleague*
colorato/a/i/e (adj)   *coloured*
colore (n) (m)   *colour*
come?   *how?*
come   *as, like*

come ...   *as ...as*
cominciare*   *to begin (see p. 79)*
commerciale/i (adj)   *business*
comodo/a/i/e (adj)   *convenient*
compatto/a/i/e (adj)   *compact*
complicato/a/i/e (adj)   *complicated*
comporre*: compongo, componi,
    compone, componiamo, componete,
    compongono   *to dial*
comprare*   *to buy (see p. 79)*
compreso/a/i/e (adj)   *included*
conferma (n) (f)   *confirmation*
confermare*   *to confirm (see p. 79)*
confusione (n) (f)   *mess*
congratulazioni   *congratulations*
conoscere*   *to know, be acquainted with
    (see p. 63)*
consegna (n) (f)   *consignment of goods*
conservare*   *to keep (see p. 79)*
consultare*   *to consult (see p. 79)*
contatto (n) (m)   *contact*
contento/a/i/e (adj)   *happy, content*
controllare*   *to check (see p. 79)*
con   *with*
coordinare*   *to coordinate (see p. 79)*
coordinatore (n) (m)   *coordinator*
copia (n) (f)   *copy*
corrispondenza (n) (f)   *correspondence*
corso (n) (m)   *course*
cosa (n) (f)   *thing*
cosa?   *what?*
costare*   *to cost (see p. 79)*
credere*   *to believe (see p. 79)*
cucina (n) (f)   *kitchen*

d'accordo   *OK*
da notare   *NB*
da parti di   *from*
da, (dal, dall', dallo, dalla)   *from,
    since/for*
danneggiamento (n) (m)   *damage*
data di scadenza (n) (f)   *expiry date*
davanti   *in front*
davvero   *really*
desidera?*   *how may I help you?*
destra   *right*
di (del, dell', dello, della)   *of*
di persona   *in person*
di solito   *usually*
diamoci del tu*   *let's use the familiar
    form when addressing each other (see
    p. 40)*
dietro   *behind*
difficile/i (adj)   *difficult*
difficoltà (n) (f)   *difficulty*
digitale/i (adj)   *digital*
dimenticare*   *to forget (see* cercare*)*
direi   *I would say*
direttamente   *directly*
direttore (n) (m)   *director*
direttore commerciale (n) (m)
    commercial director
direttore vendite (n) (m)   *sales director*
direttrice amministrativa (n) (f)
    administrative director
direzione (n) (f)   *management, direction*
direzione commerciale (n) (f)
    commercial management

direzione di produzione (n) (f)
    production management
direzione generale (n) (f)   *top
    management*
dischetto (n) (m)   *disk*
disegno (n) (m)   *design, drawing*
disponibile/i (adj)   *available*
disponibilità (n) (f)   *availability*
distinti saluti   *yours sincerely*
diventare*   *to become (see p. 79)*
diviso/a/i/e (adj)   *divided*
doccia (n) (f)   *shower*
docente (n) (m/f)   *teacher, tutor*
documento (n) (m)   *document, ID*
dolce (n) (m)   *dessert*
domani   *tomorrow*
donna (n) (f)   *woman*
doppia (n) (f)   *double room*
doppio/a/i/e (adj)   *double*
dopo   *after*
dov'è?*   *where is? (see p. 14)*
dove   *where*
dovere*: devo, devi, deve, dobbiamo,
    dovete, devono   *to have to, must*
dritto   *straight on*
dunque   *therefore, so*

e   *and*
ecco   *here is, there is*
ecologico/a/i/he (adj)   *environmentally
    friendly*
economico/a/i/he (adj)   *cheap*
edicola (n) (f)   *news-stand*
egregio/a/i/e (adj)   *distinguished*
entrata (n) (f)   *entrance*
esatto/esattamente   *exactly*
esempio (n) (m)   *example*
esperto (n) (m)   *expert*
esportare*   *to export (see p. 79)*
espresso (n) (m)   *expresso coffee*
essere*: sono, sei, è, siamo, siete,
    sono   *to be*
esterno/a/e/i (adj)   *external*
estero   *abroad*
età (n) (f)   *age*

fa   *ago*
facile/i (adj)   *easy*
famiglia (n) (f)   *family*
fare*: faccio, fai, fa, facciamo, fate,
    fanno   *to do, to make*
    fare una passeggiata   *to go for a walk*
favore (n) (m)   *favour*
    per favore   *please*
fermata (n) (f)   *bus stop*
fidanzato/a (n) (m/f)   *fiancé(e)*
fiera (n) (f)   *fair*
figlia (n) (f)   *daughter*
figlio (n) (m)   *son*
filiale (n) (f)   *branch, subsidiary company*
finalmente   *at last*
finanza (n) (f)   *finance*
finanziario/a/i/e (adj)   *financial*
fine (n) (f)   *end*
finire*: finisco   *to finish (see p. 79)*
fino a   *until*
firma (n) (f)   *signature*
fisica (n) (f) nucleare   *nuclear physics*

foglio, fogli (n) (m)   *sheet/s*
formaggio (n) (m)   *cheese*
fornire*: fornisco   *to supply (see p. 79)*
forse   *perhaps*
forte/i (adj)   *hard, strong*
fotocopiare*   *to photocopy (see p. 79)*
fotocopiatrice (n) (f)   *photocopier*
fotocopie (n) (f)   *photocopy*
francese/i (adj)   *French*
fratello (n) (m)   *brother*
frequentare*   *to attend (see p. 79)*
fumo (n) (m)   *smoke*
funzionare*   *to function, work (see p. 79)*
fuori   *outside*
    fuori sede   *off site*

gelateria (n) (f)   *ice-cream parlour*
gelato (n) (m)   *ice-cream*
generazione (n) (f)   *generation*
gentile/i (adj)   *kind*
gestire*: gestisco   *to manage (see p. 79)*
gestione (n) (f)   *business management*
giardino (n) (m)   *garden*
già   *already*
giornale (n) (m)   *newspaper*
giornata (n) (f)   *day*
giovane/i (adj)   *young*
giù   *down*
grafico (n) (m)   *graph*
grande/i (adj)   *big, large*
gratuito (adj)   *free*
grazie   *thanks*
grigio (adj)   *grey*
gruppo (n) (m)   *group*
guardare*   *to watch (see p. 79)*
guidare*   *to drive (see p. 79)*

il   *the*
illegale/i (adj)   *illegal*
illeggibile/i (adj)   *illegible*
impiegato (n) (m)   *clerk*
in   *in, at*
in comune   *shared*
in fondo   *down there, at the end*
in rapporto a   *in relation to*
incidente (n)(m)   *accident*
incontrare*   *to meet (see p. 79)*
indicare*   *to show (see p. 79)*
indice (n) (m)   *index*
indirizzo (n) (m)   *address*
indispensabile/i (adj)   *necessary*
infanzia (n) (f)   *childhood*
infatti   *in fact*
informarsi   *to get information*
    si informa   *gets information*
informatica (n) (f)   *IT*
informatizzato/a/i/e (adj)   *with
    computer skills*
informazione (n) (f)   *information*
ingegnere (n) (m)   *engineer*
inglese/i (adj)   *English, British*
ingresso (n) (m)   *entrance (ticket)*
iniziale/i (adj)   *initial*
insalata (n) (f) mista   *mixed salad*
inserire*: inserisco   *to insert (see p. 79)*
insieme   *together*
insomma   *well ...*
interessante/i (adj)   *interesting*

interessare* *to interest (see p. 79)*
interesse (n) (m) *interest*
interno (n) (m) *extension number*
interno/a/i/e (adj) *internal*
introduzione (n) (f) *introduction*
io *I*

lacerazione (n) (f) *tearing*
lasciare* *to leave (see p. 79)*
laurea (n) (f) *degree*
lavorare* *to work (see p. 79)*
lavorativo/a/i/e (adj) *working*
lavoratore (n) (m) *worker*
lavoro (n) (m) *work*
la *it, the*
lettera (n) (f) *letter*
Le *to you, to her*
lì *there*
libro (n) (m) *book*
limonata (n) (f) *lemonade*
linea (n) (f) *line*
linea telefonica (n) (f) *telephone line*
lingua (n) (f) *language*
lira (n) (f) *lira (currency)*
lo *it, the*
lontano *far*
luce (n) (f) *light*
lungo/a/hi/he (adj) *long*

ma *but*
macchina (n) (f) *car*
magazzino (n) (m) *warehouse*
  grande magazzino *department store*
male *badly*
  non c'è male *not bad*
mandare* *to send (see p. 79)*
mangiare*: mangio, mangi, mangia,
  mangiamo, mangiate,
  mangiano *to eat*
manomissioni (n) (fpl) *tampering*
massimale (n) (m) *reimbursement*
matita (n) (f) *pencil*
mattina (n) (f) *morning*
melone (n) (m) *melon*
meno . . . di . . . *less . . . than . . .*
mensa (n) (f) *canteen*
mensile/i (adj) *monthly*
mercato valutario (n) (m) *currency market*
merce (n) (f) *goods*
mese (n) (m) *month*
messaggio (n) (m) *message*
metropolitana (n) (f) *underground, tube*
mettere* *to put (see p. 79)*
mezzo/a/i/e (adj) *half*
mezzogiorno (n) (m) *midday*
mi *me*
  mi dispiace *I'm sorry*
mia, mio *my*
mila *thousands*
mille *thousand*
minestrone (n) (m) *country vegetable soup*
mito (n) (m) *myth*
mobili (n) (mpl) *furniture*
modello (n) (m) *example, model*
modificare* *to alter (see cercare)*
molto *much, very, a lot*

momento (n) (m) *moment*
moneta (n) (f) *money, change*
montagna (n) (f) *mountain*
  in montagna *to the mountains*
mostrare* *to show (see p. 79)*
moto (n) (f) *motorbike*
museo (n) (m) *museum*

nazionalità (n) (f) *nationality*
ne *of it, of them*
negozio (n) (m) *shop*
noleggiare* *to hire (see p. 79)*
noleggio auto (n) (m) *car hire*
nome (n) (m) *forename*
non *not*
nulla *nothing*
numero (n) (m) *number*
Nuova York *New York*
nuovo/a/i/e (adj) *new*

o *or*
oasi (n) (f) *nature reserve*
occupazione (n) (f) *job, work*
oggetto (n) (m) *object*
oggi *today*
ogni *every, each*
omaggio (n) (m) *small gift*
operazione (n) (f) *operation*
ora *now*
ora (n) (f) *hour*
  a che ora? *at what time?*
orario (n) (m) *times, timetable*
ordine (n) (m) *order*
organizzato/a/i/e (adj) *organised*
orientamento (n) (m) *careers guidance*
osservare* *to observe (see p. 79)*
ovunque *anywhere*

paese (n) (m) *country, nation*
pagare* *to pay (see p. 79)*
pare* *it seems*
  mi pare* *it seems to me*
parrucchiere (n) (m) *hairdresser*
partire* parto *to leave (see p. 79)*
partita (n) (f) di calcio *football match*
parziale/i (adj) *partial*
passaporto (n) (m) *passport*
passare* *to pass (see p. 79)*
passare da *to call at*
patatine (n) (fpl) *(roast) potatoes, chips*
pausa (n) (f) *pause, break*
peccato (n) (m) *shame*
  che peccato *what a shame*
penna (n) (f) *pen*
per *to, for, in order to*
  per andare a? *how do you get to?*
  per favore *please*
  per fortuna *fortunately*
  per noi *for us*
  per piacere *please*
perché *because*
  perché? *why?*
permesso? *may I?*
persona (n) (f) *person*
personale (n) (m) *staff*
pesce (n) (m) *fish*
piacere (n) (m) *pleasure, pleased to meet you*

piano (n) (m) *floor*
  pian terreno *ground floor*
piccolo/a/i/e (adj) *small*
più . . . di . . . *more . . . than . . .*
più presto *earlier*
poi *then*
politica (n) (f) *politics*
pollo arrosto (n) (m) *roast chicken*
pomeriggio (n) (m) *afternoon*
pomodoro ripieno (n) (m) *stuffed tomato*
popolato/a/i/e (adj) *populated*
porta (n) (f) *door*
portare* *to bring, to take (see p. 79)*
portiere (n) (m) *receptionist*
posto (n) (m) *place*
  posto di lavoro *position, job available*
potere*: posso, puoi, può, possiamo,
  potete, possono *to be able (see p. 63)*
pranzo (n) (m) *lunch*
pratico/a/i/he (adj) *practical*
preferire*: preferisco *to prefer (see p. 79)*
prefisso (n) (m) *telephone code*
prego *please don't mention it*
prelevare* *to withdraw (see p. 79)*
premere* *to press (see p. 79)*
prendere* *to take (see p. 79)*
prenotazione (n) (f) *booking*
presa (n) (f) *socket*
presentare* *to introduce (see p. 79)*
presto *soon, early*
  a presto *see you soon*
previsione (n) (f) *forecast*
previsto/a/i/e (adj) *provided*
primo/a/i/e (adj) *first*
primo (piatto) *first course*
problema (n) (m) *problem*
processo (n) (m) *process*
produzione (n) (f) *production*
proezione (n) (f) *projection*
professione (n) (f) *profession, job, work*
profumeria (n) (f) *perfumery*
programma (n) (m) *programme*
promozione (n) (f) *promotion*
pronto *ready, hello on phone*
proprio *really, just*
proscuitto (n) (m) *ham*
protetto/a/i/e (adj) *protected*
pubblicità (n) (f) *publicity, advertising*
pullman (n) (m) *coach*

qualcosa *something*
qualunque *any*
quando *when*
quanto/a/e/i (adj) *how much, how many?*
questo/a/i/e (adj) *this/these*
quindi *so, therefore*
qui *here*

ragazzo (n) (m) *boy (-friend)*
ragioniere (n) (m) *accountant*
reagire*: reagisco *to react (see p. 79)*
recessione (n) (f) *recession*
referenze (n) (fpl) *references*
regalo (n) (m) *present, gift*
reparto (n) (m) *section*

residuo/a/i/e (adj)   *remaining*
responsabile/i (adj)   *responsible*
riagganciare*   *to hang up (see p. 79)*
ricevitore (n) (m)   *receiver*
richiesta (n) (f)   *request*
richiesto/a/i/e (adj)   *required*
riforma (n) (f)   *reform*
ringraziare*   *to thank (see p. 79)*
ripetere*   *to repeat (see p. 79)*
risolvere*   *to solve (see p. 79)*
risotto (n) (m)   *rice dish*
   risotto alla milanese   *rice milanese-style*
rispondere*   *to reply (see p. 79)*
risposta (n) (f)   *reply*
ristorante (n) (m)   *restaurant*
ritirare*   *to pick up (see p. 79)*
ritorno (n) (m)   *return*
riunione (n) (f)   *meeting*
rosso/a/i/e (adj)   *red*

sala (n) (f)   *room*
   sala proezioni (n) (f)   *projection room*
   sala riunioni (n) (f)   *meeting room*
salmone (n) (m)   *salmon*
salutare*   *to say goodbye (see p. 79)*
sapere*: so, sai, sa, sappiamo, sapete, sanno   *to know (a fact)*
sarò*: sarà   *I will be, you, he, she, it will be (see p. 79)*
scadenza (n) (f)   *expiry*
scaffale (n) (m)   *shelf*
scegliere*   *to choose*
scelta (n) (f)   *choice*
scheda (n) (f)   *form, card*
   scheda di notificazione (n) (f)   *hotel registration slip*
schedario (n) (m)   *filing system*
schermo (n) (m)   *screen*
scientifico/a/i/he (adj)   *scientific*
scienziato (n) (m)   *scientist*
sciopero (n) (m)   *strike*
sconto (n) (m)   *discount*
scozzese/i (adj)   *Scottish*
scrittura (n) (f)   *handwriting*
scrivania (n) (f)   *desk*
scrivere*   *to write (see p. 79)*
   me lo scriva?   *could you write it down for me?*
   come si scrive?   *how is it written?*
scuola (n) (f)   *school*
se   *if*
seccatura (n) (f)   *nuisance*
secondo   *second; according to*
   secondo (piatto)   *main course*
sede (n)(f)   *office*
sedia (n)(f)   *chair*
selezione (n) (f)   *selection*
semplice/i (adj)   *simple*
sentire*   *to hear (see p. 79)*
senza   *without*
   senz'altro   *certainly*
sera (n) (f)   *evening*
serata (n) (f)   *evening*
serratura (n) (f)   *lock*
servire*   *to serve (see p. 79)*
servizi (n) (mpl)   *facilities*

servizio (n) (m) bancario   *bank service, transaction*
servizio acquisti   *purchasing department*
servizio taxi (n) (m)   *taxi service*
servizio vendite (n) (m)   *sales department*
sezione (n) (f)   *section*
sganciare*   *to lift the receiver (see p. 79)*
sì   *yes*
si   *one (pronoun)*
sicuro/a/i/e (adj)   *sure, certain*
significare*   *to mean (see cercare)*
signor (n) (m)   *Mr*
signora (n) (f)   *Mrs*
signorina (n) (f)   *Miss*
simile/i (adj)   *similar*
simpatico/a/i/he (adj)   *charming*
singola (n) (f)   *single room*
singolo/a/i/e (adj)   *single, one*
sinistra   *left*
sistema (n) (m)   *system*
situazione (n) (f)   *situation*
soldi (n) (mpl)   *money*
solito   *usual*
   di solito   *usually*
sollevare*   *to lift (see p. 79)*
solo/a/i/e (adj)   *only, alone*
soltanto   *only*
sonoro/a/i/e (adj)   *sound*
sopra   *above, on*
soprattutto   *especially, above all*
sorella (n) (f)   *sister*
sostituivo/a/i/e (adj)   *replacement*
sotto   *under, underneath*
sottrazione (n) (f)   *subtraction*
spagnolo/a/i/e   *Spanish*
sparire* sparisco   *to disappear (see p. 79)*
specializzazione (n) (f)   *specialisation*
spegnere*   *to switch off (irregular verb) (see p. 79)*
spesso   *often*
spinaci (n) (mpl)   *spinach*
sposato/a/i/e (adj)   *married*
spremuta (n) (f)   *freshly squeezed fruit juice*
stampante (n) (f)   *printer*
stanco/a/hi/he (adj)   *tired*
stare*: sto, stai, sta, stiamo, state, stanno   *to be (used mainly in idiomatic phrases)*
stasera   *this evening*
statua (n) (f)   *statue*
sterlina (n) (f)   *pound (currency)*
straniero/a/i/e (adj)   *foreign*
studente (n) (m)   *male student*
studentessa (n) (f)   *female student*
studiare*   *to study (see p. 79)*
su   *on, about*
sua, suo   *your, his, her, its*
subito   *immediately*
   subito qui   *right here*
successivo/a/i/e (adj)   *further*

tanto   *so much*
   tante belle cose   *all the very best*
tappeto (n) (m)   *carpet, rug*
tardi   *late*
tariffa (n) (f)   *charge*

tassì (n) (m)   *taxi*
tastiera (n) (f)   *keyboard*
tasto (n) (m)   *key*
   tasto invio (n) (m)   *start button*
   tasto ripetizione (n) (m)   *redial button/key*
tè (n) (m)   *tea*
teatro (n) (m)   *theatre*
telefonare*   *to telephone (see p. 79)*
telefonata (n) (f)   *telephone call*
testo (n) (m)   *text, message*
tifoso (n) (m) di calcio   *football supporter*
tipo (n) (m)   *type*
tirocinio (n) (m)   *work experience*
toccare*   *to touch (see p. 79)*
toeletta (n) (f)   *toilet*
tornare*   *to return (see p. 79)*
torta (n) (f) di verdura   *vegetable pie or flan*
trasporto (n) (m)   *transport*
tratta/si tratta   *its about*
travellers' (n) (mpl)   *travellers' cheques*
treno (n) (m)   *train*
troppo   *too*
trovare*   *to find (see p. 79)*
tu   *you (informal)*
turismo (n) (m)   *tourism*
tutto/a/i/e (adj)   *all*
   tutto bene   *everything's fine*

ufficio (n) (m)   *office*
   ufficio informazioni (n) (m)   *information office*
   ufficio magazzino (n) (m)   *warehouse office*
ultimo/a/i/e (adj)   *last*
un, una, uno   *one*
Ungheria   *Hungary*
usare*   *to use (see p. 79)*
uscire*: esco, esci, esce, usciamo, uscite, escono   *to go out*
uscita (n) (f)   *escape (computer) exit*
utile/i (adj)   *useful*
utilizzabile/i (adj)   *usable*

va bene   *OK, that's fine*
valigia (n) (f)   *suitcase*
vedere*   *to see (see p. 79)*
veloce/i (adj)   *fast*
vendita (n) (f)   *sale*
venire*: vengo, vieni, viene, veniamo, venite, vengono   *to come*
ventiquattrore (n) (f)   *briefcase*
verde/i (adj)   *green*
verificare*   *to check (see cercare)*
vero?   *isn't it, aren't you, etc.*
via (n) (f)   *street*
viaggiare*   *to travel (see p. 79)*
viaggio (n) (m)   *journey*
vino (n) (m)   *wine*
visitare*   *to visit (see p. 79)*
visivo/a/i/e (adj)   *visual*
volentieri   *willingly*
volere*: voglio, vuoi, vuole, vogliamo, volete, vogliono   *to wish, to want (see p. 63)*
volo (n) (m)   *flight*
volta (n) (f)   *time*
   una volta   *once*